Bloomsbury Professional Law Insight

AI in Criminal Law

Dr Áine Josephine Tyrrell
Barrister, Technology Policy and Law Researcher

Ben Douglas-Jones KC
5 Paper Buildings, Temple, London; and St Philips Chambers, Birmingham

Bloomsbury Professional

LONDON • DUBLIN • EDINBURGH • NEW YORK • NEW DELHI • SYDNEY

BLOOMSBURY PROFESSIONAL

Bloomsbury Publishing Plc
50 Bedford Square, London, WC1B 3DP, UK
1385 Broadway, New York, 10018, USA
Bloomsbury Publishing Ireland Ltd
29 Earlsfort Terrace, Dublin 2, D02 AY28, Ireland

First published in Great Britain 2025

2

Printed 2025, Reprinted 2025

British Library Cataloguing-in-Publication Data

A catalogue record for this book is available from the British Library.

ISBN:	PB:	978 1 52653 159 9
	Epdf:	978 1 52653 161 2
	Epub:	978 1 52653 160 5

Typeset by Evolution Design and Digital (Kent)
Printed and bound in Great Britain by CPI Group (UK) Ltd, Croydon, CR0 4YY

FSC www.fsc.org MIX Paper | Supporting responsible forestry FSC® C013604

For product safety related questions contact productsafety@bloomsbury.com

Preface

'It [is] the best of times, it [is] the worst of times, it [is] the age of wisdom, it [is] the age of foolishness, it [is] the epoch of belief, it [is] the epoch of incredulity, it [is] the season of Light, it [is] the season of Darkness, it [is] the spring of hope, it [is] the winter of despair, we [have] everything before us, we [have] nothing before us, we [are] all going direct to Heaven, we [are] all going direct the other way [...]' – Charles Dickens, from *A Tale of Two Cities*

Views on the impact that Artificial Intelligence will have – on the world and on the law specifically – range from its heralding utopia to causing the extinction of the human race. Regardless of where one falls on the spectrum, there is a general consensus that it will bring substantial changes to the rate at which work is done, the work expected of legal practitioners on a daily basis, and the types of claims we are asked to deal with.

The sheer speed of innovation in the AI space means we do not pretend to provide a definitive answer or solution to the AI-in-law question. Rather, this volume seeks to provide practitioners with: (1) a grounding in where and how the technology is already being used today; and (2) an outline of where and how it will be used in the next 5–10 years.

To this end, this short guide has a tripartite structure:

- Part 1: An Introduction to AI and Data Protection for lawyers
- Part 2: AI in Crime
- Part 3: AI in Legal Practice

Part 1 begins with an introduction to fundamental AI terms and concepts. It provides readers with a basic understanding of Foundation Models, machine learning, and Large Language Models, to name but a few concepts. This then leads into Chapter 2, an overview of existing legislation for data protection and data privacy in the United Kingdom. This chapter also looks at the obligations imposed on UK-based actors under the new EU AI Act.

Part 2 focuses on how AI is already being used to facilitate 'traditional' crimes and/or in cybercrime. Chapter 3 explores cyber crimes such as phishing and deepfakes before moving to consider dark web markets for CSAM and weaponry. This leads into Chapter 4 one how the Metropolitan Police and other authorities are using AI to improve their detection of criminal activity, to deter crimes, and/or to facilitate (and expedite) investigations.

Though last in the sequence, Part 3: AI in Legal Practice, is the beating heart of this volume. In this section we walk practitioners through the ethical and legal questions they must ask themselves before integrating AI into their criminal practice. We also provide a step-by-step guide to setting up an enterprise account with Google Gemini to ensure that all the necessary data privacy and data protection requirements are being met when using GenAI on a day-to-day basis. We then walk readers through real-world examples of how and when AI can be used in criminal practice. Finally, Part 3 considers how the judiciary – both in the UK and abroad – is already deploying AI for tasks ranging from outlining ideas through to drafting full judgements.

By way of conclusion, we turn to the future, to consider how the field of criminal law will change in the coming years and what technological developments we are likely to see and use in our day-to-day life in 5–10 years' time.

Dr Áine Josephine Tyrrell
Ben Douglas-Jones KC
February 2025

Contents

Part 1: An Introduction to AI and Data Protection for Lawyers

Chapter 1

Introduction to AI fundamentals

1.01 Whether one believes the machines are here to save us or exterminate us, the reality is that Artificial Intelligence (AI) is here to stay. Like the inventions of the wheel, the printing press, electricity, and the telephone before it, AI stands to radically transform, not only how humans go about their lives, but also how they view themselves and their relationships to each other. Needless to say, when questions of a person's responsibilities and roles in society are raised, questions regarding their rights are not far behind. In his Sir Henry Brooke Lecture for BAILII on 12 November 2019 entitled 'Algorithms, Artificial Intelligence and the Law,' Lord Sales, Justice of the UK Supreme Court, deemed it necessary for the law to engage with and adapt to this Brave New World of AI:

> 'We need to think now about the implications of making human lives subject to these processes, for fear of the frog in hot water effect. We, like the frog, sit pleasantly immersed in warm water with our lives made easier in various ways by information technology. But the water imperceptibly gets hotter and hotter until we find we have gone past a crisis point and our lives have changed irrevocably, in ways outside our control and for the worse, without us even noticing. The water becomes boiling and the frog is dead.[1]'

1.02 Before engaging with how AI is already being used, both to perpetuate crimes and as a tool by law practitioners, it is worth briefly highlighting a number of key concepts in the field of information technology. Admittedly, the degree of detail or understanding required by lawyers will vary depending on the nature of the AI system of interest, the crime perpetuated, or the lawyer's intended use for an AI system. This, therefore, is not an attempt to provide a comprehensive overview; given the speed of innovation in this sphere, such an overview would be outdated by the time this manuscript is even published. Rather, this is a gloss of concepts that all lawyers should consider so that – in the words of Lord Sales – as the water gets hotter, we not only know we have to jump, but we know what to look for once we have jumped.

1.03 There is a final vital disclaimer to make: one of the amazing and amazingly frustrating aspects of this field is that every definition provided here has been, and is still being, haggled over, disputed, argued against, argued for, and otherwise contested on a daily – if not hourly – basis.

1 Lord Sales, 'Algorithms, Artificial Intelligence and the Law,' *The Sir Henry Brooke Lecture for BAILII* (London: 12 November 2019), p.2. https://www.bailii.org/bailii/lecture/06.pdf

To try and navigate these troubled waters, we have distilled definitions from both sides of the Atlantic down to their common denominators. Where this proved impossible, we have provided a definition that seems most appropriate within the UK's legislative landscape and recent, foreign legislation (like the EU AI Act) which will impact legal practitioners in England and Wales (and beyond) in the very near future.

KEY CONCEPTS

1.04 As a starting point, academics and intergovernmental taskforces (eg EU-US Trade and Technology Council) have yet to agree upon a standard definition for 'artificial intelligence'. Loosely defined, the term refers to machines that are capable of responding to stimuli in a manner consistent with humans, given humanity's 'capacity for contemplation, judgement, and intention.'[2] There are three categories of AI – narrow, general, and super –though super intelligence AI is still in the research phase[3]. Narrow AI refers to a machine that performs a single or small number of tasks extremely efficiently. 'General AI[4]' is another term for generative AI or foundation models and describes machines capable of a wide variety of tasks and, more importantly, of moving seamlessly between said tasks similarly to how humans multitask[5].

1.05 AI can have a wider number of characteristics and capabilities, depending on the techniques used and the specifics of the use case. However, in terms of regulation, there are two key characteristics that existing regulation may not be fully suited to address: (1) the 'adaptiveness' of the technology, or the AI system's logic/ intent when performing an action; and (2) the 'autonomy' of the technology, or assigning responsibility for the AI system's action.

1.06–1.07 AI often demonstrates a high degree of autonomy, operating in dynamic and fast-moving environments by automating complex cognitive tasks. Whether that is playing a video game or navigating a vehicle on public roads, this ability to strategise and react is what fundamentally makes a system 'intelligent'. However, it also means decisions can be made without express intent or the ongoing control of a human.

1.08 This takes us to one of the big buzz terms of today: '**Machine learning**' or ML. This term refers to an algorithm's ability to classify data, text, pictures etc. without detailed instructions from a human. In so doing, it learns how to accurately predict new data points, texts, pictures

2 Shukla Shubhendu and Jaiswal Vijay, 'Applicability of Artificial Intelligence in Different Fields of Life' (Sept 2013) 1 IJSER, 28–35.

3 IBM Data and AI Team, 'AI vs. Machine Learning vs. Deep Learning vs. Neural Networks: What's the difference?,' *IBM Blog*, published 6 July 2023 < https://www.ibm.com/blog/ai-vs-machine-learning-vs-deep-learning-vs-neural-networks/>

4 M. Estévez Almenzar et al. 'Glossary of human-centric artificial intelligence,' European Commission: *Joint Research Center,* 2022, pp. 32.

5 John R. Allen and Darrell M. West, 'The Brookings glossary of AI and emerging technologies,' *Brookings Institute,* published 13 July 2020 < https://www.brookings.edu/articles/the-brookings-glossary-of-ai-and-emerging-technologies/#_edn1>

etc based on 'learned' information[6]. A prime example is Amazon's use of ML to recommend products to users based on what they have previously browsed and/or purchased on the platform.

1.09 ML that is not 'deep' learning requires human intervention to teach the computer how to identify patterns or to perform specific tasks, and to do so accurately and consistently[7]. Thus, human programmers determine what characteristics distinguish a group of images, texts, or tasks in a series or what labels to assign to each unit within a series. If a series of images of different flatbreads featured injera, pita, and dosa, the human may teach the machine that the characteristic distinguishing one image from the next is the type of flour used. Alternatively, they may choose to label the images 'injera', 'pita', and 'dosa' so that the machine will recognise similar images in the future.

1.10 Another commonly used term is '**neural network**'. The term refers to a subfield of machine learning that is heavily inspired by how the neurons function in our human brains. Our brain cells form an interconnected network that works together to solve a given problem, with neurons communicating to each other using electrical signals. Similarly, the neurons that make up an artificial neural network, work together to solve a given problem[8]. Artificial neurons are small units or modules of computer software – called '**nodes**'[9]; when taken together to form the overall artificial neural network, these nodes form a software program or algorithm that, in essence, uses computing systems to solve mathematical equations[10]. **'Deep' neural networks** refers to the fact that neural networks can have multiple layers. A basic neural network has an input layer, hidden layer, and an output layer[11]. The input layer receives data, processes it, and passes it to the hidden layer, which then analyses the data emitted by the input layer, processes it, and passes it to the output. Deep neural networks, however, can have large numbers of interconnected hidden layers whereby each one takes the output from the previous hidden layer, processes it further, and then passes it onto the next (hidden) layer[12].

1.11 Meanwhile, '**Deep learning**' differs from non-deep ML in that it does not require a labelled data set to learn the relationships between data in a set. It can use statistics to spot underlying trends and patterns in unprocessed data and then applies these trends to new data independently[13]. Deep learning AI is trained on '**big data**' – large, complex data sets that are

6 Dorian Pyle and Cristina San Jose, 'An Executive's Guide to Machine Learning,' McKinsey Quarterly, June, 2015.
7 IBM Data and AI Team, 'AI vs. Machine Learning vs. Deep Learning vs. Neural Networks: What's the difference?,' *IBM Blog,* published 6 July 2023 < https://www.ibm.com/blog/ai-vs-machine-learning-vs-deep-learning-vs-neural-networks/>
8 'What is a neural network?' *Amazon Web Services,* https://aws.amazon.com/what-is/neural-network/#:~:text=A%20neural%20network%20is%20a,that%20resembles%20the%20human%20brain.
9 'What is a neural network?' *Amazon Web Services,* https://aws.amazon.com/what-is/neural-network/#:~:text=A%20neural%20network%20is%20a,that%20resembles%20the%20human%20brain.
10 'What is a neural network?' *Amazon Web Services,* https://aws.amazon.com/what-is/neural-network/#:~:text=A%20neural%20network%20is%20a,that%20resembles%20the%20human%20brain.
11 'What is a neural network?' *Amazon Web Services,* https://aws.amazon.com/what-is/neural-network/#:~:text=A%20neural%20network%20is%20a,that%20resembles%20the%20human%20brain.
12 'What is a neural network?' *Amazon Web Services,* https://aws.amazon.com/what-is/neural-network/#:~:text=A%20neural%20network%20is%20a,that%20resembles%20the%20human%20brain.
13 'What is Deep Learning,' *IBM* < https://www.ibm.com/topics/deep-learning>

stored, analysed, and processed by high-computing powered machines[14]. As the machine parses through more and more data, it becomes increasingly capable of determining abstract patterns across data points and, therefore, able to perform tasks with increasing accuracy. These systems are sometimes referred to as '**autonomous AI systems**' as they can perform tasks, modify their own objectives, and alter their own *modus operandi* independently of human oversight or other external interventions[15].

1.12 With Chat-GPT's rise in popularity, most people have become familiar with the term '**Language model**'. These are algorithms based on natural language processing, a machine's ability to 'process, analyse and mimic human language'[16]. In other words, they capture patterns and syntactical rules of language which they then use to make assumptions and to apply the rules to previously unseen text. **Large Language models** (LLMs) (like ChatGPT) are a subcategory of language models that use deep-learning and that are trained on big data[17]. There are two categories of LLMs: generative and discriminatory. Generative models can generate original text in answer to a prompt (write an essay or answer a question etc). They can be unsupervised (no human intervention) – like ChatGPT – or semi-supervised (requiring minimal human intervention). Discriminatory LLMs are supervised models and are typically used to classify text – for example, to determine if something was written by a human or an AI[18].

1.13 This brings us to the term foundation model (or FM). The Stanford Center for Research on Foundation Models (CRFM) – the centre which first coined the term – defines these as being, 'general-purpose technologies or platforms for products and applications, including generative AI'[19]; they are AI systems that can generate compelling text, images, and more. In simplistic terms, one model is trained on a huge amount of data so that it can be adapted to many applications. One of the best known examples of an FM is OpenAI's ChatGPT but other examples include Anthropic's Claude, Microsoft Copilot, or Google's Gemini. The type of data used to train the model determines the 'model' of the FM. Thus, large language models are predominantly trained on text data, image generation models on image data, and multi-modal FMs on more than one data type[20].

---

14 EU-U.S. Terminology and Taxonomy for Artificial Intelligence,' *European Commission* published 31 May 2023 < https://digital-strategy.ec.europa.eu/en/library/eu-us-terminology-and-taxonomy-artificial-intelligence>

15 M. Estévez Almenzar et al. 'Glossary of human-centric artificial intelligence,' European Commission: *Joint Research Center,* 2022, pp. 15.

16 EU-U.S. Terminology and Taxonomy for Artificial Intelligence,' *European Commission* published 31 May 2023 < https://digital-strategy.ec.europa.eu/en/library/eu-us-terminology-and-taxonomy-artificial-intelligence>

17 EU-U.S. Terminology and Taxonomy for Artificial Intelligence,' *European Commission* published 31 May 2023 < https://digital-strategy.ec.europa.eu/en/library/eu-us-terminology-and-taxonomy-artificial-intelligence>

18 EU-U.S. Terminology and Taxonomy for Artificial Intelligence,' *European Commission* published 31 May 2023 < https://digital-strategy.ec.europa.eu/en/library/eu-us-terminology-and-taxonomy-artificial-intelligence>

19 'Response to AI Accountability Policy Request for Comment,' *Center for Research on Foundation Models,* 12 June 2023 < https://hai.stanford.edu/sites/default/files/2023-06/Response-to-Request.pdf>

20 'AI Foundation Models: Initial Report,' *Competition & Markets Authority,* 18 September 2023 < https://assets.publishing.service.gov.uk/government/uploads/system/uploads/attachment_data/file/1185508/Full_report_.pdf> p.8.

1.14 The CRFM at Stanford has described the complexity of FMs as an ecosystem with three categories of assets: (1) **Resources** or data (eg, the billions of words and images on the Internet) and computation (eg, through cloud providers like Amazon, Google, and Microsoft) necessary for training foundation models; (2) **Foundation models**, such as ChatGPT Diffusion; and (3) **Products and services atop these models** (eg, Bing Search, Khan Academy's Khanmigo AI-powered tutor). They underscore that it is this third category of assets that determines much of the digital supply chain and, therefore, the interrelationships and dependencies between organisations (eg Khan Academy depends on OpenAI because GPT-4 powers Khanmigo13)[21].

1.15 According to the Competition and Markets Authority (CMA), the development of (generative) AI models is limited by a number of factors relating to compute, data, and expertise. '**Compute**' refers to the network of computers necessary for processing the vast amounts of data required to power AI models. Compute is required to: (1) train models to learn patterns and logic; (2) power an AI system to make real-time decisions; and (3) reduce latency thus providing users with a smooth user-experience[22]. Like AI, there is no single definition of the term 'compute' but, broadly, it refers to three components: (1) the metric measurement of the number of operations a computer processor can handle in one second (known as floating-point operations per second or FLOPS); (2) the physical hardware – computer chips – that perform the calculations and data processing; and (3) a 'stack' of three components that work together to power an AI system, namely the hardware (chips), software (programming language/code used), and the infrastructure (data centres, servers, cables, cooling systems etc)[23]. Most AI developers rely on cloud service providers including Amazon, Microsoft, and Google, to access the necessary compute resources.

WHY SHOULD WE CARE?

1.16 In 2018, OpenAI released the Generative Pre-trained Transformer (GPT) or GPT-1, the first publicly available large language foundation model (LLM), a watershed moment in publicly available LLMs.[24] While in 2023, it was estimated that approximately 160 foundation models (FMs) had been developed and released publicly, globally,[25] the Stanford CRFMs estimates that over 120 FMs were released between Sept 2023 and March 2024 alone, bringing the number of known FMs to over 300[26]. Indeed, foundation models are the fastest-growing consumer

21 'Response to AI Accountability Policy Request for Comment,' *Center for Research on Foundation Models,* 12 June 2023 < https://hai.stanford.edu/sites/default/files/2023-06/Response-to-Request.pdf> p. 3.
22 Aadya Gupta and Adarsh Ranjan, 'A Primer on Compute,' *Carnegie Endowment for International Peace* (30 April 2024) <https://carnegieendowment.org/posts/2024/04/a-primer-on-compute?lang=en>
23 Aadya Gupta and Adarsh Ranjan, 'A Primer on Compute,' *Carnegie Endowment for International Peace* (30 April 2024) <https://carnegieendowment.org/posts/2024/04/a-primer-on-compute?lang=en>
24 'What are Foundation Models?' *Generative AI with AWS,* AWS Amazon.com < https://aws.amazon.com/what-is/foundation-models/>.
25 *AI Foundation Models: Summary,* Competition & Markets Authority, 18 September 2023 < https://assets.publishing.service.gov.uk/government/uploads/system/uploads/attachment_data/file/1185505/Summary_.pdf>
26 Stanford CRFM (2023) Ecosystem Graphs for Foundation Models. <https://crfm.stanford.edu/ecosystem-graphs/index.html?mode=table>

technology in human history with the Financial Times reporting more than $11 billion USD being directed towards developing foundational model start-ups in Q1 of 2023.

1.17 In the UK specifically, Ofcom's research into the AI sector has revealed that 31% of adults and 79% of 13–17 year olds living in the UK have used a generative AI tool such as ChatGPT[27]. Similarly, the UK Office for National Statistics (ONS) has concluded that 15% of UK businesses are already using at least one form of AI; this number is significantly higher for larger businesses with 46% reporting using AI to 'improve business operations', 'provide or personalise a product or service', and 'develop a new product or service or explore a new market'.[28] Meanwhile, the UK Government's 'Artificial Intelligence sector study 2022' surveyed companies registered and with an active presence in the UK; they found that there were 3,170 active AI companies in the UK in 2022, which generated £10.6 billion in AI-related revenue.[29]

1.18 Unsurprisingly, policymakers worldwide have only increased their efforts to grapple with (generative) AI. Domestic examples of policy interventions are the UK's Department of Science, Innovation and Technology's (DSIT) *Algorithmic Transparency Recording Standard*[30] and AI Management Essentials tool[31], the Government Digital Service's Artificial Intelligence (AI) Playbook for the UK Government[32], and the CMA's study of how best to guide the development of FMs[33]. Abroad, approaches have ranged from the introduction of formal legislation (eg the EU's Artificial Intelligence Act[34]) through to the promotion of voluntary Codes of Conduct (eg the US's AI Bill of Rights[35]).

---

27 Ofcom (2023) Online Nation 2023 Report <https://www.ofcom.org.uk/siteassets/resources/documents/research-and-data/online-research/online-nation/2023/online-nation-2023-report.pdf?v=368355>

28 ONS (2024) Business insights and impact on the UK economy, Wave 98 (published in February 2024, reference period of November 2023) <https://www.ons.gov.uk/economy/economicoutputandproductivity/output/datasets/businessinsightsandimpactontheukeconomy>

29 'Artificial Intelligence Sector Study,' *Research report for the Department for Science, Innovation and Technology (DSIT)*, March 2023 < https://assets.publishing.service.gov.uk/government/uploads/system/uploads/attachment_data/file/1145582/artifical_intelligence_sector_study.pdf>, pp.7

30 'Algorithmic Transparency Recording Standard Hub', *Department for Science, Innovation and Technology, GOV.UK*, <https://www.gov.uk/government/collections/algorithmic-transparency-recording-standard-hub>

31 'AI Management Essentials', Department for Science, Innovation and Technology, GOV.UK, https://www.gov.uk/government/consultations/ai-management-essentials-tool

32 https://gds.blog.gov.uk/2025/02/10/launching-the-artificial-intelligence-playbook-for-the-uk-government/.

33 'Foundation Models: Update paper', *Competition Market Authority, GOV.UK*,(16 April 2024) <https://www.gov.uk/government/publications/ai-foundation-models-update-paper>

34 Regulation (EU) 2024/1689 of the European Parliament and of the Council of 13 June 2024 laying down harmonised rules on artificial intelligence and amending Regulations (EC) No 300/2008, (EU) No 167/2013, (EU) No 168/2013, (EU) 2018/858, (EU) 2018/1139 and (EU) 2019/2144 and Directives 2014/90/EU, (EU) 2016/797 and (EU) 2020/1828 (Artificial Intelligence Act), <https://eur-lex.europa.eu/legal-content/EN/TXT/?uri=OJ:L_202401689>

35 'Blueprint for an AI Bill of Rights,' *Office of Science and Technology Policy*, US White House <https://www.whitehouse.gov/ostp/ai-bill-of-rights/>

Chapter 2

An introduction to UK data protection law for/in AI

2.01 As mentioned in the previous Chapter, (generative) AI developers are typically limited in their ability to innovate by three factors: expertise, data, and compute. With this context, it is important for legal practitioners to note that: (1) developers predominantly access compute via partnerships with cloud service providers and/or strategic investments; (2) developers are accessing data via partnerships with proprietary data sources (eg publishers) or licensing deals, and (3) FM models are not only being released but are being integrated into other products, particularly commonly used digital products and services, meaning the market is evolving towards greater monetisation[1]. Though seemingly disparate, these three interrelationships necessitate answering the same legal questions: who owns the data; who has the right to process the data; can the data be stored and, if so, for how long; what can the data be used for; how is data protected; and how was consent secured from the data subjects involved? In short, the success of the AI sector depends upon data privacy and data protection principles.

2.02 Despite GenAI's importance for the economy and society, not to mention the US and EU's eagerness to introduce AI regulations, the previous Government was reluctant to introduce new legislation regulating AI[2]. Its White Paper, published in March 2023, made clear the Conservative Party believed it too soon to make cross-sectoral decisions on liability in the AI supply chain. Instead, it adopted a 'contextual, sector-based regulatory framework', anchored in its existing regulators and laws[3]. Though the present Labour government has pledged to introduce an AI Bill to formally regulate AI[4], the existing regulatory landscape will prevail until Parliament passes such an Act.

2.03 While the Labour Government has made their commitment to regulating AI known – as evidenced by their release of the AI Playbook for the UK Government – there is still ambiguity surrounding if and how these commitments will translate into hard legislation. Thus, this chapter will begin by exploring the obligations placed on AI deployers under current legislation. We

1 'Foundation Models: Update paper', *Competition Market Authority, GOV.UK,*(16 April 2024) <https://www.gov.uk/government/publications/ai-foundation-models-update-paper>

2 UK Department for Science, Innovation & Technology, *A pro-innovation approach to AI regulation* (CP 815, 2023).

3 Ada Lovelace Institute, 'Regulating AI in the UK' (July 2023). < https://www.adalovelaceinstitute.org/report/regulating-ai-in-the-uk/> accessed 23 October 2023.

4 Harry Booth, 'What We Know About the New U.K. Government's Approach to AI,' *Time Magazine* (12 July 2024) <https://time.com/6997876/uk-labour-ai-kyle-starmer/>

will then discuss the Information Commissioner's Office's (ICO) strategic approach[5] and explicit guidelines[6] for ensuring AI remains data protection-compliant under the UK GDPR. These guidelines offer insight into how the ICO applies data protection law to AI while demonstrating how data-driven AI must comply with data protection principles 'by design and by default[7]'. By way of conclusion, we will provide an overview of recent developments in UK policy regarding AI and touch on what experts believe Labour is likely to prioritise in its forthcoming legislation.

OVERVIEW OF THE UK GDPR

2.04 UK data subjects' rights are protected by the **Data Protection Act (DPA) 2018** in conjunction with the **UK General Data Protection Regulation (UK GDPR)**[8]. As the name would suggest, the DPA and the UK GDPR were passed to integrate the EU's GDPR stipulations into British law. Similar to its EU counterpart, the UK GDPR not only establishes standards for data protection but imposes obligations on any organisation that works with or collects data from, about, or otherwise related to UK residents, regardless of whether or not the company is based in the UK.

2.05 The principles underpinning the DPA and the UK GDPR are set out in UK GDPR, Article 5(2): lawfulness, fairness, and transparency; purpose limitation; data minimisation; accuracy; storage limitation; integrity and confidentiality; and accountability[9]. For example, **Article 5(1)(a)** of the UK GDPR requires a person's personal data to be processed 'lawfully, fairly and in a transparent manner in relation to the data subject ("lawfulness, fairness and transparency")'. While 'data subject' is used to refer to the individual whose data is being processed, 'processing' is defined in **Article 4(2)** as being any operation performed on data –whether or not this storage, collection, transmission, or any other use is automated[10]. Transparency is further unpacked in **Recital 58** which requires any information 'addressed to the public or data subject to be concise, easily accessible and easy to understand [...]' An interconnected obligation is that organisations may not deceive or mislead data subjects regarding how or why their data is being processed[11]. **Recital 60** requires a processor to inform data subjects of the existence of any profiling and its consequences. **Articles 12 to 22** provide data subjects with various protections including the right to be informed, to access their data, to erasure, and the right to restrict processing.[12]

5 *Regulating AI: The ICO's Strategic Approach* (April 2024) Information Commission Office <https://www.skadden.com/-/media/files/publications/2024/05/the-uk-ico-publishes-its-strategy-on-ai-governance/regulating-ai-the-icos-strategic-approach.pdf?rev=7752a638c485400fb9e1e84dbe077ab6&hash=16CEEC36DAF5CD2A68D4F7A14F30A401>
6 'About this Guidance,' (ICO.org.uk, 2023) < https://ico.org.uk/for-organisations/uk-gdpr-guidance-and-resources/artificial-intelligence/guidance-on-ai-and-data-protection/about-this-guidance/#whatdoyou> accessed 19 September 2023.
7 'Is this guidance a set of AI principles?' (ICO.co.uk, 2023) < https://ico.org.uk/for-organisations/uk-gdpr-guidance-and-resources/artificial-intelligence/guidance-on-ai-and-data-protection/about-this-guidance/#whatdoyou> accessed 19 September 2023.
8 Part 2 of the DPA 2018 is responsible for tailoring the UK GDPR.
9 Ch 2, Art 5 United Kingdom General Data Protection Regulation 2016.
10 Art 4(2) UK GDPR.
11 Recital 60 UK GDPR.
12 Ch 3 Art 12-22 United Kingdom General Data Protection Regulation 2016.

2.06 As regards automated data collection and processing specifically, **Article 22(1)** protects data subjects' right to not be subjected to a decision that is, 'based solely on automated processing [...] which produces legal effects concerning him or her or similarly affects him or her.' The exceptions, per **Article 22(2)** are: if there is a contract in place between the data subject and a data controller, the data subject has given explicit consent, or if the collecting and processing of the subject's data is required/ authorised by domestic law.[13]

2.07 These (non-exhaustive) protections and data rights result in obligations for data controllers and processors that are codified in Chapter IV of the UK GDPR. A **controller** is defined as the natural or legal person or body that 'determines the purposes and means of the processing of personal data.[14] A **processor**, meanwhile, is a natural or legal person or body that processes personal data on a controller's behalf[15]. The cornerstone of the processors' responsibilities is the idea that data protection must be 'by design and by default[16]. Under **Article 24**, appropriate technical and organisational measures must be adopted before, during, and after data processing to meet the UK GDPR's requirements and protect data subjects' rights. Moreover, by default, only personal data that is strictly necessary for the specific purpose of the processing shall be collected, processed, stored, and accessed. Similarly, the processor has obligations to process the personal data transferred to them by the controller while adhering to the UK GDPR principles – in terms of the technical and organisational measures they employ[17]. Under **Article 30**, both bodies are required to maintain records of all processing activities that fall under their respective responsibilities, including: the purposes of the processing, a description of the technical and organisational security measures put in place to safeguard data rights, and the categories of persons to whom the data has and/or will be disclosed[18].

OVERVIEW OF THE EU AI ACT (EU AIA)

2.08 Unlike the UK, the European Union has developed a comprehensive law for regulating the development, deployment and use of AI. It is worth quickly summarising the main premises of the EU Artificial Intelligence Act 2024 ('EU AI Act' or 'EU AIA') because organisations or legal practitioners that have EU operations or use AI systems that process/ use EU citizens' data in any way are likely to be subject to the EU AIA's edicts. This is particularly true given the Labour party's forthcoming legislation is unlikely to deviate significantly from what the EU has introduced; though they are eager to avoid succumbing to the Brussels effect, they will continue to adhere to OECD principles[19] and other international commitments in the interest of trade and

13 Art 22 United Kingdom General Data Protection Regulation 2016.
14 Art 4(7) UK GDPR.
15 Art 4(8) UK GDPR.
16 Art 25(1) UK GDPR.
17 Art 28 UK GDPR.
18 Art 30 UK GDPR.
19 OECD AI Principles <https://oecd.ai/en/ai-principles>

diplomacy. It is important for UK actors, therefore, to determine whether or not they require an AI governance framework that is compatible with the EU's principles.

2.09 The EU AIA is the first piece of legislation comprehensively to regulate the creation, deployment, and use of AI systems. The Act was passed by the EU Parliament in December 2023 and came into force on 1 August 2024.[20] The Act is built on the European Commission's risk-based approach to AI; it establishes four levels of risk for AI systems and identifies a number of risks specific to existing general purpose AI models. The four categories of risk outlined are:

1. **Minimal risk**: AI systems that are sufficiently regulated by existing legislation and, therefore, can be developed and used without additional obligations placed on the provider. Most AI systems will fall under this category.
2. **High risk**: AI systems that could potentially have an adverse impact on people's safety or their fundamental rights. High risk obligations also apply to safety components of products. This category is defined in further detail below.
3. **Unacceptable risk**: The EU has created an exhaustive list of particularly harmful uses of AI that are banned because they contravene EU values:
    - Social scoring
    - Exploitation of vulnerable persons and/or use of subliminal techniques
    - Real-time remote biometric identification in publicly accessible spaces by law enforcement (subject to narrow restrictions);
    - Biometric categorisation of people based on biometric data to deduce their race, political opinions, religious beliefs, sexual orientation etc.
    - Individual predictive policing;
    - Emotion recognition in the workplace and in educational institutions (unless for safety reasons); and
    - Untargeted scraping of the internet or CCTV for facial images for the purpose of compiling or expanding a database.
4. **Specific Transparency risk**: certain systems will be subject to specific transparency requirements where there is a clear risk of manipulation. Users of these systems should always be made aware that they are interacting with an AI.

2.10 AIA also addresses '**systemic risks**' that might arise from the use or deployment of GPAIs, including large generative AI models (foundation models).

20 Directorate-General for Communication, 'AI Act enters into force,' *European Commission* (1 August 2024) <https://commission.europa.eu/news/ai-act-enters-force-2024-08-01_en#:~:text=On%201%20August%202024%2C%20the,and%20deployment%20in%20the%20EU>.

2.11 As previously stated, the EU AIA will apply to both public and private actors that put an AI system on the EU market or create and/or deploy a system that affects people located in the EU. Where the actors in question are located does not matter: actors located outside the EU will have to comply with AIA if their AI system is sold in the EU or if, when deployed, it impacts those living in the EU. Given this, AIA will impact UK actors who export AI systems to the EU or who deploy systems that, when used, will affect people living in the EU.

2.12 Deloitte[21] has compiled a very clear table breaking down the different responsibilities for AI providers and AI deployers. Providers of high-risk AI systems **must**:

1 Complete a conformity assessment prior to placement of system on the market and/or use of system. Providers must also complete a new conformity assessment every time the system is substantially updated or modified OR if the purpose for which the system is being used materially changes;

2 Register their system in the newly created EU AI database;

3 Comply with the EU AIA's rules for: Data quality and governance; Transparency; Accuracy, robustness, and cybersecurity; Human oversight; Risk and quality management systems; Technical documentation; Record keeping;

4 Implement a post-market monitoring system and a system for incident reporting.

2.13 Deployers of high-risk AI systems **must**:

1 Complete a fundamental rights impact assessment (this only applies to certain deployers/use cases – see **2.16** below);

2 Comply with the provider's instructions regarding technical and organisational measures for their AI system;

3 Assign human oversight to competent, trained, and well-supported personnel;

4 Ensure that the input data used by the system is relevant and representative for the AI system's intended purpose;

5 Fulfil all monitoring, record-keeping, and incident reporting obligations, both to providers and to the relevant EU/national authorities.

2.14 The conformity assessment (at Art 3(20)) is intended to demonstrate that the AI system being provided and/or deployed meets the mandatory requirements for trustworthy AI stipulated in Chapter II, Section 2 of AIA (eg data quality, documentation and traceability, transparency, accuracy, human oversight etc). As previously intimated , both providers and deployers of high-risk systems will have to implement quality and risk management processes to ensure that they

21 Suchitra Nair & Valeria Gallo, 'The EU AI Act: the finish line is in sight', *Deloitte* (10 June 2024) <https://www2.deloitte.com/uk/en/blog/emea-centre-for-regulatory-strategy/2023/the-eu-ai-act-the-finish-line-is-in-sight.html>

not only comply with AIA's requirements but also minimise risks for users by applying necessary corrective or preventive actions, **even after the product/system is placed on the market** (as per Art 3(25); Art 72).

2.15 Most AI systems – including those produced or deployed in the UK – fall under the 'minimal risk' category, and the provisions in Chapter 2 of AIA currently only apply to high risk systems. However, deployers and providers of minimal risk AI systems will be required to comply with transparency obligations for all AI systems that interact with natural persons or that generate content. These requirements are designed to prevent human manipulation or deception. They will also be strongly encouraged to adopt approved codes of conduct. Moreover, it is highly likely that some of the Chapter 2 obligations will be made compulsory for lower risk systems in the near future. Indeed, even in its current iteration, AIA encourages providers of minimal risk systems to apply the requirements for trustworthy AI and to voluntarily develop codes of conduct for the development or deployment of an AI system.

HOW AIA BUILDS ON/REINFORCES RIGHTS AND OBLIGATIONS IN THE GDPR

2.16 AIA explicitly states that its provisions should be implemented without prejudice to existing data protection mechanisms and frameworks in the European union. EU AIA describes itself as 'complementary' to existing legislation (at [9] in the Preamble). At [10] in the Preamble, the EU AIA explicitly points to the GDPR as the keystone protection of personal data,' and underscores that it 'does not seek to affect the application of existing Union law governing the processing of personal data, including the tasks and powers of the independent supervisory authorities competent to monitor compliance with those instruments.' This is further stated in Art 1(7) of EU AIA. AIA is expressly predicated on ethical principles for trustworthy AI (developed by the independent AI HLEG in 2019); many of these principles echo those underlying the GDPR framework. The synergies between the underlying principles of these two pieces of legislation is most evident in the AIA's Preamble. The importance of transparency and access to high quality data, as well as the implementation of appropriate data governance and management practices, are emphasised at [67]. The GDPR is also explicitly cited as the authority for data protection in the EU. Subsequent paragraphs continue to refer to the other GDPR principles, for example: data minimisation and data protection by design and default are cited at [69]; protections of special categories of personal data are referred to at [70]; and accountability and transparency underlie the emphasis placed on traceability of high risk systems at [72].

2.17 Art 10 details the data governance required for high risk AI systems; it specifies that training, validation and testing data shall be subject to practices geared towards ensuring the data sets are 'sufficiently representative' and appropriate or complete 'in view of the intended purpose'. The language used throughout Art 10 evokes the GDPR's 'data protection by design and default,' in that high risk system providers must have a view to the possible biases that are likely to negatively impact the fundamental rights, health and/or safety of persons when designing the data sets, the system's architecture, and underlying assumptions of their systems. This is most evident in subsection 5(5) where the Act lists specific conditions that must be met if AI high-risk system providers wish to process special categories of personal data for bias detection and correction purposes (these are listed in Art 5(5)). These data requirements correlate to the GDPR principles:

1 Art 5(5)(a) requirements correspond to GDPR principle of lawfulness;

2 Art 5(5)(b) and (c) correspond to GDPR principles of integrity and confidentiality, and purpose limitation;

3 Art 5(5)(d) corresponds to GDPR principle of confidentiality;

4 Art 5(5)(e) corresponds to GDPR principle of storage limitation;

5 Art 5(5)(f) corresponds to GDPR principle of accountability.

2.18 Art 12 of AIA prescribes record-keeping processes that must be built into high-risk systems: such systems must 'technically allow for the automatic recording of events over their lifetime.' This emphasis on documentation and traceability recalls Art 30 of the GDPR as this article, too, was designed to ensure that an adequate standard of accountability for and traceability of data processing is upheld by data controllers. Art 30 of the GDPR refers to records of data processing activities; it states that each controller and, where applicable, the controller's representative, shall maintain a record of processing activities under its responsibility. Records such include, among other things, the purposes of the processing, description of the categories of data subjects and of personal data and categories of recipients to whom the personal data has been/will be disclosed.

UK VS EU AIA: DIFFERENCES IN THE APPROACHES

2.19 Unsurprisingly, there is a number of AI-related activities or risks that current UK regulations and/or practices do not cover which are, instead, addressed in the EU AIA. However, the need for secondary EU legislation in key areas, and/or the need for standards to be formally defined by third parties and EU bodies means the shortfall is not as significant as may seem at first blush.

2.20 This being said, one of the crucial differences between AIA and the UK's approach is that, in Articles 85–87, it provides various remedies to natural or legal persons with grounds to believe that there has been an infringement of AIA or of their fundamental rights due to the use of an AI system. Art 85 refers to the right to lodge a complaint with a market surveillance authority if they believe there has been an infringement of AIA's provisions. These complaints are to be handled in accordance with the complaint/reporting procedures market surveillance authorities already have in place. Art 86 protects an individual's right to an explanation if affected by a decision taken by a deployer based on output from a high-risk system listed in Annex III of AIA *and* the decision in question produced legal effects or similarly significantly impacted the complainant in such a way that they consider it to have had an adverse impact on their health, safety, or fundamental rights. Under Art 86(1) they have the right to obtain clear and meaningful explanations as to the role the AI system played in the decision-making process that impacted them; as well as an overview of the main elements of the decision that was taken. However, Art 86(2) seems to provide significant exemptions to this protection: it does not apply to the use of AI systems for which exemptions/restrictions follow from other EU legislation or national law. The implication here is that, should Member States' domestic laws restrict or exempt a certain use of AI systems from the obligation to provide an explanation, then the consumer or complainant does not have recourse for seeking further information under AIA. Art 87 states that those who report AIA infringements are protected under the Directive (EU) 2019/1937 on the protection of persons who report breaches of Union law[22].

2.21 For its part, the EU AIA does not address the two key issues faced by AI developers (in the EU and worldwide): (1) how to train their AI systems without violating data protection, copyright or personality rights; and (2) how to access high-quality datasets. Admittedly, the EU Commission is developing guidelines for EU AI developers for implementing the EU AI Act including a blueprint of the various relevant rules in different EU laws (eg AI Act, GDPR, Data Act, DGA, Copyright Directive). They will also be complemented by a harmonised set of procedures (eg points of contact, deadlines), common interpretations of certain processes (eg standardised guidance for how to anonymise, pseudomise, or use synthetic data), and a new understanding of Art 6(4) of the GDPR as it pertains to training algorithms and training data sets (eg how purpose limitation applies, reducing the focus on 'consent' and the obligation to inform). Given the complexity of the legal issues surrounding copyright infringement and personal data protections in big data sets used for training and/or used by models with continuous learning architectures, there are serious concerns about the economic viability, clarity, and/or practical feasibility of these forthcoming guidelines. To this point, the very architecture of the open internet and of GPAIs means that, once data is fed into the model, it cannot easily be removed or 'extracted[23]'. The detangling process would require a combination of technical and legal solutions, something that seems ambitious given the tight timeframes for implementation of these measures and/or the lack of specificity around financial support to be offered Small and Medium Enterprises (SMEs), start-ups, and public bodies seeking to comply with AIA's obligations.

22 Directive (EU) 2019/1937 of the European Parliament and of the Council of 23 October 2019 on the protection of persons who report breaches of Union law <https://eur-lex.europa.eu/legal-content/EN/TXT/?uri=CELEX%3A02019L1937-20240311>

23 See: Stanford University paper on 'Foundation Models and Copyright Questions' for techniques that could be used to mitigate against copyright infringement in GPAIs.

CONCLUSION: REGULATORS AND THE FUTURE OF AI REGULATION

2.22 Although multiple regulators have published reports and provided guidance regarding AI, the ICO has played a particularly notable role with some arguing it has risen to be the *de facto* regulator for AI in the UK[24]. This influence stems from the fact that the previous Conservative Government's principles for AI, as articulated in the 2023 White Paper[25], mapped onto the statutory principles the ICO already oversees under the UK GDPR and the DPA 2018. The White Paper principles were, broadly: safety and security; appropriate transparency and explainability; fairness; accountability; and contestability and redress; all of these echo the emphases placed on integrity, security, fairness, accountability, transparency, accuracy etc. in data protection law.

2.23 As previously intimated, the current Labour Government has announced a fundamental shift from a principles-based approach to explicit, centralised regulation of AI. It intends to introduce 'binding regulation' on companies developing generative AI models[26]. In terms of data protection, while their election manifesto committed to improving data sharing across public services and to creating a 'National Data Library' for delivering data-drive public services, it was largely silent on data protection reform[27]. It is unclear, therefore, whether they will revive the Data Protection and Digital Information Bill proposed by the Conservative Party to revise the UK GDPR; when it was originally proposed, many Labour party members were supportive of the Bill[28] but no mention of data protection reform has been made, in the King's Speech or other fora, since the General Election.

2.24 This being said, the Labour Government has launched a number of 'soft' policy frameworks for companies and public bodies. These are intended to help them (self) regulate how they develop and/or deploy AI in their workflows. For example, the Department for Science, Innovation and Technology (DSIT) launched the *AI Management Essentials* tool in November 2024[29]. The tool is designed for any organisation that develops, provides or uses services that utilise AI systems as part of their operations and is sector agnostic[30]. It distils key principles from existing AI regulations, standards, and frameworks – including ISO/IEC 42001, the NIST Risk

24 David A. Simon et al. 'The UK ICO Publishes Its Strategy on AI Governance,' *Skadden Publication – AI Insights* (13 May 2024) <https://www.skadden.com/insights/publications/2024/05/the-uk-ico-publishes-its-strategy-on-ai-governance>

25 *A pro-innovation approach to AI regulation,* White Paper (August 2023) UK Government <https://www.gov.uk/government/publications/ai-regulation-a-pro-innovation-approach/white-paper>

26 Change – Labour Party Manifesto 2024 (2024) <https://labour.org.uk/wp-content/uploads/2024/06/Labour-Party-manifesto-2024.pdf> p.35

27 Change – Labour Party Manifesto 2024 (2024) <https://labour.org.uk/wp-content/uploads/2024/06/Labour-Party-manifesto-2024.pdf> p.35

28 Debbie Heywood, 'Labour sets out its stall – UK AI, data and cyber security legislation announced in King's Speech,' *TaylorWessing* (18 July 2024) <https://www.taylorwessing.com/en/insights-and-events/insights/2024/07/radar-uk-ai-data-and-cybersecurity-legislation-announced-in-kings-speech>

29 In the interest of transparency, Dr Tyrrell was a team lead for the development of AIME and was the lead author of the tool's content until September 2024.

30 *Open Consultation: Guidance for using the AI Management Essentials Tool* <https://www.gov.uk/government/consultations/ai-management-essentials-tool/guidance-for-using-the-ai-management-essentials-tool> (6 November 2024).

Management Framework, and the EU AI Act. The aim is to 'provide an accessible resource for organisations to assess and improve their AI management systems and practices[31].' According to DSIT's recent report, *'Assuring a Responsible Future for AI,'* AIME is merely the first of many 'soft power' frameworks and tools developed by Government to mitigate the risks associated with AI and drive demand for a UK-based AI assurance market[32]. Indeed, most recently, the Government Digital Service launched its AI Playbook, designed to support civil servants and public bodies as they integrate AI into their workflows.

31 *Guidance for using the AI Management Essentials tool* <https://www.gov.uk/government/consultations/ai-management-essentials-tool/guidance-for-using-the-ai-management-essentials-tool> (6 November 2024).

32 *Assuring a Responsible Future for AI* <https://www.gov.uk/government/publications/assuring-a-responsible-future-for-ai/assuring-a-responsible-future-for-ai#:~:text=We%20will%20drive%20demand%20for,including%20an%20AI%20Essentials%20Toolkit.

Part 2: AI in Crime

Chapter 3

How AI is being used in/for criminal activities

3.01 The explosion of generative AI apps, add-ons, and plug-ins in recent years has brought with it a wave of new art forms[1], coding capabilities[2], writing tools[3], and video content[4]. AI powered chatbots have even reached the point of sophistication that they can emulate human conversational patterns and interact with humans with ease, responding to questions and manoeuvring from topic-to-topic without issue[5]. However, the ability to generate code or create audio, video, images and documents from straightforward prompts presents criminals with new opportunities and/or the tools to commit old crimes in new ways.

3.02 Given the limited scope of this book, we will limit our discussion to three ways in which AI is already being used in/ for criminal activity – in the UK and abroad:

1 Deepfakes;

2 Phishing attacks;

3 Cybercrime.

DEEPFAKES

3.03 Deepfakes[6] are highly realistic, entirely fabricated images, video or other media, created using genAI. These manipulated or fictitious videos, photographs, or audio recordings can be used for a variety of malicious purposes:

1 Eric Zhou, Dokyun Lee, Generative artificial intelligence, human creativity, and art, *PNAS Nexus*, Volume 3, Issue 3, March 2024, pgae052, https://doi.org/10.1093/pnasnexus/pgae052

2 'AI code generation,' *Google Cloud* <https://cloud.google.com/use-cases/ai-code-generation?hl=en>

3 'AI Writing Tools for Effortless Writing,' *Grammarly.com* <https://www.grammarly.com/ai-writing-tools>

4 Bernard Marr, '5 Generative AI Video Tools Everyone Should Know About,' (14 February 2024) *Forbes.com* <https://www.forbes.com/sites/bernardmarr/2024/02/14/5-generative-ai-video-tools-everyone-should-know-about/>

5 'AI Chatbot,' *Google Cloud* <https://cloud.google.com/use-cases/ai-chatbot?hl=en>

6 Deepfakes are created using two elements: 1) compute known as Generative Adversarial Networks (GANs); and 2) a huge amount of data. GANs are a type of AI algorithm made of two neural networks: a generator and a discriminator. The 'generator' analyses a huge amount of data about the target person – learning their facial features, voice tone, inflections, and movements – and uses this information to create fake content; it superimposes the target person's likeness onto a source video or source photograph. The 'discriminator' assesses the 'fake' content against 'real' data about the subject being 'deepfaked'. The discriminator then analyses the fake footage or images against the originals and identifies where the 'fake' diverges from the 'real' data. It feeds this information back into the generator so that a new iteration of more realistic fake content can be generated. With each iteration/ interplay between generator and discriminator, the deepfake becomes more realistic. Source: Sara H. Jodka, 'Manipulating reality: the intersections of deepfakes and the law,' (1 February 2024) *Reuters.com* <https://www.reuters.com/legal/legalindustry/manipulating-reality-intersection-deepfakes-law-2024-02-01/>

- **Extortion and blackmail:** criminal entities can fabricate compromising camera footage, audio, or photographs and use them as leverage to extort money or other favours from their victims[7].
- **Identity theft/fraud:** criminals can create deepfakes to impersonate individuals and/or to commit fraud[8].
- **Fake news:** deepfakes can be used to create fake news stories for a variety of purposes, including influencing popular elections[9].

Extortion and blackmail

3.04 Deepfakes most often take the form of sexually explicit content. Like phishing, the use of deepfakes pre-dates publicly available or open-source generative AI; reports show Reddit forum users were superimposing female celebrities' faces into pornographic footage as far back as 2017[10]. With the rise of AI tools such as Dall-E 3[11], anyone can create an extreme, violent, or sexual fantasy in seconds. Research has shown that content is typically accompanied by misogynistic, transphobic, homophobic language (depending on the gender or sexual orientation of the subjects) intended to try and silence, intimidate, or dehumanise the individuals 'represented' in the images[12].

3.05 Alarmingly, young people and women are increasingly falling victim to scams in schools and the workplace. Some of the most notorious examples of AI-generated deepfake blackmail and bullying were linked to the Clothoff deepfake pornography app[13]. The app invites users to 'undress anyone using AI' for approximately £8.50 a month for 25 credits; the credits are used to upload photographs of women and girls which are then returned with the subjects stripped of their clothing[14]. The incident came to public attention after it was reported that children –

7 'New laws criminalise the sharing of intimate deepfakes without consent,' (5 February 2024) *Refuge.org.uk* <https://refuge.org.uk/news/new-laws-criminalise-the-sharing-of-intimate-deepfakes-without-consent/>

8 Kennedy Meda, 'Identity theft is being fueled by AI & cyber-attacks,' (3 May 2024) *Thomson Reuters* <https://www.thomsonreuters.com/en-us/posts/government/identity-theft-drivers/>

9 Marina Adami, 'How AI-generated disinformation might impact this year's elections and how journalists should report on it,' (15 March 2024) *Reuters Institute, Oxford University* <https://reutersinstitute.politics.ox.ac.uk/news/how-ai-generated-disinformation-might-impact-years-elections-and-how-journalists-should-report>

10 Emine Saner, 'Inside the Taylor Swift deepfake scandal: 'It's men telling a powerful woman to get back in her box,' *The Guardian UK* (31 January 2024) <https://www.theguardian.com/technology/2024/jan/31/inside-the-taylor-swift-deepfake-scandal-its-men-telling-a-powerful-woman-to-get-back-in-her-box>

11 https://openai.com/index/dall-e-3/

12 Emine Saner, 'Inside the Taylor Swift deepfake scandal: 'It's men telling a powerful woman to get back in her box,' *The Guardian UK* (31 January 2024) <https://www.theguardian.com/technology/2024/jan/31/inside-the-taylor-swift-deepfake-scandal-its-men-telling-a-powerful-woman-to-get-back-in-her-box>

13 Reuters in Madrid, 'Spanish prosecutor investigates if shared AI images of naked girls constitute a crime,' (25 September 2023) *The Guardian UK* <https://www.theguardian.com/world/2023/sep/25/spanish-prosecutor-investigates-if-shared-ai-images-of-naked-girls-constitute-a>

14 Michael Safi, Alex Atack, and Joshua Kelly, 'Revealed: the names linked to ClothOff, the deepfake pornography app,' *The Guardian UK* (29 February 2024) <https://www.theguardian.com/technology/2024/feb/29/clothoff-deepfake-ai-pornography-app-names-linked-revealed>

particularly young girls – in Spain[15] and New Jersey[16] were being targeted by explicit deepfake images generated by students in their class using the app. In an interview about the impact of deepfakes on young women, Rani Govender, senior policy and public affairs officer at the NSPCC, remarked: '[T]his [imagery] is sent around schools and used as a form of sexual harassment and bullying. Fear is a theme that comes up a lot: worrying that people will think it's real, that it can lead to further sexual harassment and bullying. [There is] worry about what their parents might think[17].' As a result of the investigation conducted for The Guardian's podcast series, *Black Box*[18], access to the app was blocked in the UK but remains available abroad.

3.06 This case points to the fact that millions of people are targeted by deepfakes on a daily basis. A 2019 study conducted by Deeptrace found that 96% of online deepfake video content was non-consensual pornography[19]. Aside from bullying, the images are often also created as part of a grooming process, to threaten children, or to share and sell to sexual offenders[20]. The impacts of these images cannot be overstated, particularly as takedown and removal of the images is futile – it is virtually impossible to guarantee complete removal once an image is posted online.

Identity theft and fraud

3.07 The first instance of AI-powered fraud occurred in 2019, when scammers used an AI generated voice clip of an energy group CEO to direct the CEO of its UK subsidiary to release EUR 230,000 to a fictitious Hungarian supplier[21]. Since then, GenAI powered tool such as VALL-E[22] and ElevenLabs[23] have only become more adept at simulating human voices: even just a voicemail recording or a short clip scraped from Tik Tok is enough for the software to accurately emulate people's vocal patterns[24]. Regula, a global developer of forensic devices and identity

15 Michael Safi, Alex Atack, and Joshua Kelly, 'Revealed: the names linked to ClothOff, the deepfake pornography app,' *The Guardian UK* (29 February 2024) <https://www.theguardian.com/technology/2024/feb/29/clothoff-deepfake-ai-pornography-app-names-linked-revealed>

16 Tim McNicholas, 'New Jersey high school students accused of making AI-generated pornographic images of classmates,' *CBS News* (2 November 2023) <https://www.cbsnews.com/newyork/news/westfield-high-school-ai-pornographic-images-students/>

17 Emine Saner, 'Inside the Taylor Swift deepfake scandal: 'It's men telling a powerful woman to get back in her box,' *The Guardian UK* (31 January 2024) <https://www.theguardian.com/technology/2024/jan/31/inside-the-taylor-swift-deepfake-scandal-its-men-telling-a-powerful-woman-to-get-back-in-her-box>

18 ' Black Box,' (February – March 2024) *The Guardian UK <https://www.theguardian.com/technology/series/blackbox>*

19 *The State of Deepfakes: Landscape, Threats, and Impact,* (September 2019) Deeptrace <https://regmedia.co.uk/2019/10/08/deepfake_report.pdf>

20 Emine Saner, 'Inside the Taylor Swift deepfake scandal: 'It's men telling a powerful woman to get back in her box,' *The Guardian UK* (31 January 2024) <https://www.theguardian.com/technology/2024/jan/31/inside-the-taylor-swift-deepfake-scandal-its-men-telling-a-powerful-woman-to-get-back-in-her-box>

21 Catherine Stupp, 'Fraudsters Used AI to Mimic CEO's Voice in Unusual Cybercrime Case,' *WSJ* (30 August 2019) <https://www.wsj.com/articles/fraudsters-use-ai-to-mimic-ceos-voice-in-unusual-cybercrime-case-11567157402>

22 https://www.microsoft.com/en-us/research/project/vall-e-x/

23 https://elevenlabs.io/text-to-speech?utm_source=google&utm_medium=cpc&utm_campaign=uk_nonbrandsearch_voicegen_english&utm_id=20740063169&utm_term=ai%20voice%20generator&utm_content=voicegen_exact&gad_source=1&gclid=Cj0KCQiA6Ou5BhCrARIsAPoTxrCnUhpJMhyQRIEyQb3kzIUYzXSZA8-Az_BTtG_F-lh7KqSqsdMHS_EaAvUIEALw_wcB

24 Megan Cerullo, Cybercriminals are using AI voice cloning tools to dupe victims, (21 March 2023) *CBS News* <https://www.cbsnews.com/news/ai-scam-voice-cloning-rising/>

verification solutions, found that 37% of organisations surveyed globally have experienced some kind of deepfake voice fraud attempt[25].

Fake news

3.08 Deepfakes are also used to generate sexually explicit content and fake news stories targeting public figures. For example, in February 2024, sexually explicit AI-generated images of Taylor Swift were posted on X[26]. In the 17 hours the images were live, they received 45 million views, 24,000 reposts, and hundreds of thousands of likes and bookmarks[27]. Needless to say, the virality of the images meant the post caused significant damage – emotional, reputational, etc – to Swift, despite their being removed within 24 hours. Similarly, the rise in AI-generated 'revenge porn' led the UK government to criminalise the sharing of 'deepfake' intimate images[28]. This crime will be introduced into law as an amendment to the Criminal Justice Bill[29] criminalising the creation of horrific or sexually explicit images without consent; creators are to be made liable regardless of whether they create the image(s) with the intent to disseminate or not[30].

3.09 Outside of producing and disseminating sexually explicit fake news, deepfakes can also be used to manipulate political opinion or social stability via false reports and misinformation. For example, they have been used to fabricate videos or audio recordings of politicians saying or doing things they never did. In the UK, Labour's Wes Streeting was targeted by a political smear campaign on X involving a deepfake video of him calling a BBC Politics Live presenter a 'silly woman'.[31] Deepfakes can be used to sow discord among different groups, leading to social unrest or violence and the undermining of geo-political systems[32]. Two extreme examples of this phenomenon are: (1) a deepfake featuring the late Indonesian dictator, Suharto, in which he 'delivered' a message to voters ahead of the election in February 2024[33]; and (2) the Pizzagate news story that circulated at the time of the US 2016 Presidential election[34].

---

25 'Press Release: One-Third of Global Businesses Already Hit by Voice and Video Deepfake Fraud,' *Regula Forensics.com* (27 April 2023) <https://regulaforensics.com/news/one-third-of-global-businesses-already-hit-by-voice-and-video-deepfake-fraud/>

26 Emily Saner, 'Inside the Taylor Swift deepfake scandal: 'It's men telling a powerful woman to get back in her box,' *The Guardian UK* (31 January 2024) <https://www.theguardian.com/technology/2024/jan/31/inside-the-taylor-swift-deepfake-scandal-its-men-telling-a-powerful-woman-to-get-back-in-her-box>

27 Sarah H. Jodka, 'Manipulating Reality: the intersection of deepfakes and the law,' *Reuters* (1 February 2024) <https://www.reuters.com/legal/legalindustry/manipulating-reality-intersection-deepfakes-law-2024-02-01/>

28 Pranshu Verma and Gerrit De Vynck, 'AI is destabilising the 'concept of truth itself' in 2024 election,' *The Washington Post* (22 January 2024) <https://www.washingtonpost.com/technology/2024/01/22/ai-deepfake-elections-politicians/>

29 Criminal Justice Bill, (updated 3 June 2024) *Parliament.uk* <https://bills.parliament.uk/bills/3511>

30 ' Press release: Government cracks down on 'deepfakes' creation,' (16 April 2024) *GOV.UK* <https://www.gov.uk/government/news/government-cracks-down-on-deepfakes-creation>

31 Marianna Spring, 'Labour's Wes Streeting among victims of deepfake smear network on X,' *BBC News* (7 June 2024) <https://www.bbc.com/news/articles/cg33x9jm02ko>

32 Bobby Chesney and Danielle Citron, 'Deep Fakes: A Looming Challenge for Privacy, Democracy, and National Security,' *California Law Review* Vol 107 (2019), <https://heinonline.org/HOL/LandingPage?handle=hein.journals/calr107&div=51&id=&page=>, pp.1753

33 See: Heather Chen, 'AI 'resurrects' long dead dictator in murky new era of deepfake electioneering, *CNN News* (11 February 2024) <https://www.cnn.com/2024/02/12/asia/suharto-deepfake-ai-scam-indonesia-election-hnk-intl/index.html>

34 BBC Trending, 'The saga of 'Pizzagate': The fake story that shows how conspiracy theories spread,' *BBC News* (2 December 2016) <https://www.bbc.com/news/blogs-trending-38156985>

Other legal challenges posed by deepfakes

3.10 The following is a short list of some of the key legal issues associated with this technology:

1 **Intellectual Property Infringement**[35]:

- *Copyright Violations*: Deepfakes may infringe on the copyright of the original content used to create them.
- *Trademark Infringement*: Deepfakes can be used to create fake endorsements or advertisements that infringe on trademarks.

2 **International Law/Cross-Border Issues**: Deepfakes can be created and distributed across international borders, making it difficult to enforce laws and prosecute offenders.

PHISHING ATTACKS

3.11 Phishing attacks are a form of social engineering that trick individuals into clicking on malicious links or opening attachments that lead to malware infections, identity theft, or financial loss. Admittedly, **email phishing** is hardly a new phenomenon. This sort of scam sees fraudsters or hackers emailing individuals – via their private email accounts or their professional email addresses associated with companies – to entice them into making transactions that benefit the criminal (eg buying Apple gift cards or sending a Nigerian prince £10,000) or to offer up personal data that facilitates another kind of crime (getting you to hand over your personal passwords or credentials to your workplace's database). The common denominator across these criminal activities is that the scams appear to be from genuine sources and require the recipient to provide secure data in direct response to the email or by clicking on a link that redirects them to a bogus website.

3.12 Cambridge-based cybersecurity firm Darktrace has warned that since the release of ChatGPT, it has seen an increase in the linguistic complexity (in terms of the volume of text, punctuation and sentence length used) in suspicious emails targeting their customers[36]. As generative AI is increasingly being utilised to construct more sophisticated phishing scams, Darktrace have seen a concomitant decrease in the number of manipulative emails which rely on the relatively primitive method of tricking victims into clicking malicious links.

3.13 The damage resulting from successful phishing scams (eg customer data loss) can impact reputation, market position, and bring regulatory scrutiny. Developments in phishing

35 'Deepfakes and copyright protections,' *The Metropolitan Police UK* https://www.met.police.uk/advice/advice-and-information/deepfakes/deepfakes-and-copyright-protections/

36 Quinn Owen, 'How AI can fuel financial scams online, according to industry experts,' ABC News, published 12 October 2023 < https://abcnews.go.com/Technology/ai-fuel-financial-scams-online-industry-experts/story?id=103732051#:~:text=Generative%20AI%20tools%20can%20make,else's%20activity%20in%20order%20to>

sophistication pose greater challenges for those developing defences and staff training to recognise these attacks.

3.14 AI-generated phishing scams are not just more efficacious but are also more efficient for the cybercriminal. For example, the ongoing *CopyRh(ight) adamantys* campaign combines personalisation and impersonation with spamming (extremely high volume of attacks). The cyberhackers responsible are using dedicated gmail accounts to distribute emails impersonating legitimate organisations to claim that individuals or companies have violated copyright laws on their social media accounts[37]. Their process is entirely automated. Their AI system creates a new gmail account impersonating a legitimate organisation and then scrapes information about the target from their social media accounts, etc. The AI then composes a customised email: the inclusion of individualised information about the target means their fictitious claims of supposed copyright violation are as credible as possible. The AI system then sends the email to the intended victim before moving on to the next person.

3.15 In brief, the AI system can perform the following tasks effectively and at scale:

1. **Personalisation:** AI can analyse vast amounts of data to create highly personalised phishing emails that are tailored to the specific interests, preferences, and vulnerabilities of individual targets. This makes the emails more likely to be perceived as legitimate and acted upon.
2. **Natural Language Processing (NLP):** AI-powered NLP can generate more convincing and human-like phishing emails, making it harder for recipients to identify them as fraudulent.
3. **Automation:** AI can automate the creation and distribution of phishing emails at a massive scale, overwhelming victims with a barrage of attacks.
4. **Real-Time Adaptation:** AI can analyse the effectiveness of phishing campaigns in real-time and adjust the messages accordingly, making them even more effective.

CYBERCRIME

3.16 AI has significantly enhanced the capabilities of cybercriminals, enabling them to launch more sophisticated and effective attacks. Here are some ways AI is being used for cybercrime:

Malware development, botnets and Distributed Denial of Service (DDoS) attacks

3.17 AI can be used to create new and sophisticated malware variants at a rapid pace, making it difficult for security software, white-hat hackers, and/or researchers to keep up. Cybersecurity

---

37 David Winder, 'Cyber Attack Warning As Hackers Use AI and Gmail In New Campaign,' (7 November 2024) *Forbes* <https://www.forbes.com/sites/daveywinder/2024/11/07/cyber-attack-warning-as-hackers-use-ai-and-gmail-in-new-campaign/>

experts call malware source combined with LLMs 'polymorphic malware[38]'. This technology has a number of characteristics, including:

- **Mutation:** the malware can autonomously modify its own code each time it attacks a computer network, making it extremely difficult for traditional cybersecurity measures to identify and protect against it[39];
- **Obfuscation and encryption:** malware will employ a variety of techniques – including encryption, instruction substitution, etc – to hide its true purpose;
- **Amplified attacks:** AI can be used to coordinate botnets, large networks of compromised devices, to launch massive Distributed Denial of Service (DDoS) attacks (defined below) that can overwhelm websites and networks[40].

3.18 Malware, short for malicious software, is any software designed to harm a computer system or network. It can come in many forms, including: viruses, ransomware, and spyware. It can spread through various methods, including:

- **Email attachments:** malicious attachments can be sent as part of phishing emails;
- **Malicious links:** clicking on malicious links can lead to malware infections;
- **USB/USB-C drives:** infected USB and USB-C drives can spread malware to connected computers.

3.19 According to the UK's National Cyber Security Centre (NCSC), AI will make cyber attacks against the UK more impactful because malicious actors will be able to analyse exfiltrated data more effectively. Moreover, the barrier to entry for novice criminals, hackers-for-hire, and hacktivists is getting lower every year (if not every week) as hacking tools are increasingly intuitive to use and freely available on the open and dark webs.[41] Indeed, the need for these actors to code their own spy- and malware is decreasing, particularly as regards low-sophistication attacks like phishing scams. Meanwhile, there has been a rise in hacking or 'ransomware-as-a-service' whereby more capable actors are monetising their ability to coordinate and launch sophisticated attacks. Specialised criminal groups like REvil and GandCrab sell their ability to develop and launch sophisticated malware through affiliates on the dark web[42]. This business is highly lucrative: for example, IBM Security X-Force estimates that REvil's profits from their ransomware engagements and affiliate partnerships in 2023 totalled around $81 million

38 Dena De Angelo, 'The Dark Side of AI in Cybersecurity – AI-Generated Malware,' (15 May 2024) *Palo Alto Networks Blog* <https://www.paloaltonetworks.com/blog/2024/05/ai-generated-malware/>

39 Dena De Angelo, 'The Dark Side of AI in Cybersecurity – AI-Generated Malware,' (15 May 2024) *Palo Alto Networks Blog* <https://www.paloaltonetworks.com/blog/2024/05/ai-generated-malware/>

40 Jamison Utter, 'The Machine War Has Begun: Cybercriminals Leveraging AI in DDoS Attacks,' (24 September 2024) *A10 Networks.com* <https://www.a10networks.com/blog/the-machine-war-has-begun-cybercriminals-leveraging-ai-in-ddos-attacks/>

41 'The near-term impact of AI on the cyber threat,' *National Cyber Security Centre* (24 January 2024) <https://www.ncsc.gov.uk/report/impact-of-ai-on-cyber-threat#section_1>

42 Darren Guccione, 'What is the dark web? How to access it and what you'll find,' *CSO Online.com* (2 April 2024) <https://www.csoonline.com/article/564313/what-is-the-dark-web-how-to-access-it-and-what-youll-find.html>

USD[43]. Given this, it is unsurprising that the NCSC believes the national (and global) threat of ransomware will increase exponentially over the next two years.

3.20 As mentioned above, a botnet is a network of compromised devices – such as computers, smartphones, or Internet of Things devices – that are controlled by a malicious actor. These devices are infected with malware that allows the attacker to remotely command and control them. Botnets can be used for a variety of malicious purposes such as for launching DDoS attacks.

3.21 A DDoS attack is a cyberattack that aims to disrupt or deny service to a targeted system or network by overwhelming it with traffic from multiple sources; they aim to cause the loss of availability of part or all of a system[44]. They are the most prevalent form of network disruption attack and, as such, one of the largest risks to cybersecurity[45]. These attacks can cause significant financial losses for businesses and organisations and/or can damage the organisation's reputation, leading to loss of customer trust and confidence. There are three principle forms of DDoS attacks[46]:

- **Volume-based DDoS attacks**: These attacks aim to overwhelm a target's bandwidth or processing power by flooding it with a massive amount of traffic.
- **Protocol-based DDoS attacks**: These attacks exploit vulnerabilities in network protocols to disrupt the target's services.
- **Application-layer DDoS attacks**: These attacks target specific applications or services running on the target system.

Deepfakes and identity theft

3.22 As mentioned above, deepfakes can be used to create realistic videos or audio recordings of individuals, making it easier for criminals to impersonate them and defraud victims.

It is worth mentioning **synthetic identity fraud** (SIF) at this juncture. According to Thomson Reuters, synthetic fraud is one of the fastest-growing financial crimes and is almost exclusively powered by AI[47]. Indeed, a recent survey of 500 fraud and risk professionals surveyed by

43 Darren Guccione, 'What is the dark web? How to access it and what you'll find,' *CSO Online.com* (2 April 2024) <https://www.csoonline.com/article/564313/what-is-the-dark-web-how-to-access-it-and-what-youll-find.html>

44 'Denial of Service (DoS) guidance,' *National Cyber Security Centre* <https://www.ncsc.gov.uk/collection/denial-service-dos-guidance-collection>

45 Bindu Bala and Sunny Behal, 'AI techniques for IoT-based DDoS attack detection: Taxonomies, comprehensive review and research challenges,' *Computer Science Review,* Vol 52 (May 2024) <https://www.sciencedirect.com/science/article/abs/pii/S1574013724000157>

46 Bryson Medlock, 'Different types of DDoS attacks: how to protect your clients,' (10 August 2023) *Connectwise.com* <https://www.connectwise.com/blog/cybersecurity/types-of-ddos-attacks>

47 Michael Purcell, 'Synthetic Identify Fraud: What is it and How to Combat it,' *Thomson Reuters* (28 April 2023) <https://legal.thomsonreuters.com/blog/synthetic-identity-fraud-what-is-it-and-how-to-combat-it/>

ABC News demonstrates mounting concern over the growing popularity of AI-generated synthetic fraud scams[48].

3.23 SIF is much harder to address than more traditional modes of identity theft because criminals are now combining publicly available data scraped off social media and other internet sources with real (stolen) data, like a national insurance number, to manufacture their identities and avoid detection[49].

3.24 Perpetrators of SIF start with a single piece of legitimate personal data – usually a social security number – and build a fake identity around it using a bogus address, phone number, and other basic information. Fraudsters then use the fictitious identity to open lines of credit, secure vehicle loans, or scam government agencies in order to intercept tax returns and benefits payouts.

We have, in short, entered an era of 'super-charged' AI fraud, where generative AI can act more quickly and more systematically than a person. Whereas a 'traditional' fraudster's activities were constrained by their own ingenuity and basic needs (eating, sleeping etc), these constraints no longer exist in the age of generative AI.

3.25 Why has SIF taken off?

1 Somewhat ironically, security improvements in the use of physical credit cards has driven fraudsters to SIF. The introduction of EMV-chip security in debit and credit cards has made it more difficult for thieves to commit fraud in person, so they are finding ever more creative ways to steal money online.

2 Efforts to digitise almost all financial transactions, including government benefits, have created both temptation and opportunity for cyber-thieves. It is much easier to impersonate someone online than it is in person, especially if the 'person' exists only as a collection of data points. Banking, credit, and government agencies only check a few key pieces of data to establish a person's identity, and thieves are adept at mimicking them.

3 A record number of data breaches across all sectors of the economy has exposed more personal information than ever to potential criminals. According to the Identity Theft Resource Center in the US, there were 1,579 data breaches in 2017, which exposed almost 179 million personal records, including 14.2 million credit-card numbers and 158 million social security numbers. Many of these records now circulate on the dark web, where they are sold like any other commodity, to anyone who is willing to pay.

---

48 Quinn Owen, 'How AI can fuel financial scams online, according to industry experts,' ABC News, published 12 October 2023 < https://abcnews.go.com/Technology/ai-fuel-financial-scams-online-industry-experts/story?id=103732051#:~:text=Generative%20AI%20tools%20can%20make,else's%20activity%20in%20order%20to>

49 Quinn Owen, 'How AI can fuel financial scams online, according to industry experts,' ABC News, published 12 October 2023 < https://abcnews.go.com/Technology/ai-fuel-financial-scams-online-industry-experts/story?id=103732051#:~:text=Generative%20AI%20tools%20can%20make,else's%20activity%20in%20order%20to>

DARK WEB OPERATIONS

3.26 The dark web[50] is a portion of the internet that is not indexed by search engines like Google or Bing. It is commonly associated with criminal activity, though the dark web does have a number of legitimate goods and services on offer such as BlackBook, a social network known as the 'Facebook of Tor[51]'. Tor is a specific browser (like Safari or Google Chrome), albeit one that anonymises the user: it routes all web page requests a user types into their search bar through a number of proxy servers operated by thousands of volunteers around the world that help render the user's IP address untraceable and utterly anonymous[52]. The anonymity of the dark web has only increased thanks to bitcoin, the crypto-currency predicated on the complete anonymity of the buyer and seller; dark web commerce uses bitcoin – or analogous crypto currency – as legal tender[53].

3.27 The following is a non-exhaustive list of illegal activities that are carried out on the dark web:

A Illegal marketplaces[54]:

- Drug Trafficking: A significant portion of the dark web is dedicated to the sale of illegal drugs, including narcotics, prescription medications, and synthetic drugs.
- Weapons and Explosives: Dark web marketplaces also offer a variety of weapons, including firearms, explosives, and hacking tools.
- Stolen Data: Stolen personal and operational/financial information, such as credit card details, company financial records, login credentials, and social security numbers, is frequently traded on the dark web.
- Counterfeit Goods: Counterfeit products, including luxury goods, electronics, and pharmaceuticals, are also available for purchase on the dark web.

B Hacking services:

- Zero-day exploits[55]: hackers are selling zero-day exploits – cyberattacks that take advantage of vulnerabilities or flaws in software/ hardware. The 'Zero-day' refers to the fact that the developer of the computer system or software has zero days to fix the issue as malicious actors can already exploit the vulnerability.

---

50 For further information on the Dark web, see: Darren Guccione, 'What is the dark web? How to access it and what you'll find,' *CSO Online.com* (2 April 2024) <https://www.csoonline.com/article/564313/what-is-the-dark-web-how-to-access-it-and-what-youll-find.html>

51 Darren Guccione, 'What is the dark web? How to access it and what you'll find,' *CSO Online.com* (2 April 2024) <https://www.csoonline.com/article/564313/what-is-the-dark-web-how-to-access-it-and-what-youll-find.html>

52 Darren Guccione, 'What is the dark web? How to access it and what you'll find,' *CSO Online.com* (2 April 2024) <https://www.csoonline.com/article/564313/what-is-the-dark-web-how-to-access-it-and-what-youll-find.html>

53 Darren Guccione, 'What is the dark web? How to access it and what you'll find,' *CSO Online.com* (2 April 2024) <https://www.csoonline.com/article/564313/what-is-the-dark-web-how-to-access-it-and-what-youll-find.html>

54 Violeta Lyskoit, 'Darknet market: What you should know about dark web marketplaces,' (18 April 2024) *NordVPN*.com <https://nordvpn.com/blog/darknet-market/>

55 'What is a zero-day exploit?' *IBM.com* <https://ibm.com/topics/zero-day>

- Hacking-as-a-Service (HaaS)[56]: Criminals can hire hackers to launch cyberattacks on specific targets.

C Extortion and blackmail:

- Data extortion[57]: Hackers can extort money from individuals or organisations by threatening to release sensitive data that they have stolen on a data leak site, on the dark web.
- Cyber blackmail[58]: Deepfakes and other forms of manipulated media can be used to directly contact and blackmail individuals or organisations.

D Child Exploitation:

Unlike in other markets, child exploitation markets on the dark web are not necessarily for-profit. Estimates suggest only about 7.5% of content is sold for financial gain because most of the industry operates on a barter system whereby images are collected and traded within peer-to-peer networks[59].

- Child Pornography: The dark web is a hub for the distribution of child pornography: the Internet Watch Foundation has identified that AI is being used to create synthetic images and videos of child sexual abuse on the dark web[60].
- Child Trafficking: Dark web marketplaces can be used to facilitate the trafficking of children for sexual exploitation[61].

E Generative AI-Tools to automate crime:

AI has also benefited more 'traditional' operations on the dark web by allowing malicious actors to automate the operation of dark web marketplaces. WormGPT[62] was among the first such tools; it appeared in July 2023 and is marketed as a 'blackhat' alternative to ChatGPT. In other words, this LLM has no ethical boundaries, was allegedly trained on malware data, and has a range of features including unlimited character inputs, memory retention, and the ability to code[63]. Similarly, FraudGPT is a LLM marketed as an 'advanced bot for offensive purposes.'[64] It too can be used to write malicious code, create undetectable malware

56 William Self, 'Hackers for hire: The dark web, pen tests, and beyond,' (30 August 2023) *Crowe.com* <https://www.crowe.com/cybersecurity-watch/hackers-for-hire>

57 'What is a Dark Web Leak Site?' *Palo Alto Network* <https://www.paloaltonetworks.co.uk/cyberpedia/what-is-a-dark-web-leak-site>

58 Malcolm Higgins, 'Cyber extortion: What is it and how to protect yourself,' (11 January 2024) *NordVPN* <https://nordvpn.com/blog/cyberextortion/>

59 Roberta Ligget, 'Commercial Child Sexual Abuse Markets on the Dark Web', *White Paper – Michigan State University* <https://cj.msu.edu/_assets/pdfs/cina/CINA-White_Papers-Liggett_Commercial_Child_Sexual_Abuse_Markets_Dark_Web.pdf>

60 '2024 Update: Understanding the Rapid Evolution of AI-Generated Child Abuse Imagery,' (2024) *IWF.org* <https://www.iwf.org.uk/about-us/why-we-exist/our-research/how-ai-is-being-abused-to-create-child-sexual-abuse-imagery/>

61 'Dark web child abuse forum administrators jailed,' (19 February 2024) *CPS.gov.uk* <https://www.cps.gov.uk/cps/news/dark-web-child-abuse-forum-administrators-jailed>

62 Daniel Kelley, 'WormGPT – The Generative AI Tool Cybercriminals Are Using to Launch Business Email Compromise Attacks,' *Slashnext* (13 July 2023) <https://slashnext.com/blog/wormgpt-the-generative-ai-tool-cybercriminals-are-using-to-launch-business-email-compromise-attacks/>

63 Arun KL, 'The Dark Side of AI – wormGPT, a Malicious GPT Tool for Cybercriminals' *TheSecMaster.com* (23 November 2023) <https://thesecmaster.com/blog/the-dark-side-of-ai-wormgpt-a-malicious-gpt-tool-for-cybercriminals>

64 Rakesh Krishnan, 'FraudGPT: The Villain Avatar of ChatGPT,' *Netenrich.com* (25 July 2023) <https://netenrich.com/blog/fraudgpt-the-villain-avatar-of-chatgpt>

or other hacking tools, write phishing or scam content, and find security vulnerabilities in cyber systems[65]. Experts believe that, while Fraud GPT is aimed at creating quick, high-volume phishing attacks, WormGPT is geared towards creating sophisticated malware and ransomware attacks.

WormGPT and FraudGPT are merely the best known and first iterations of LLMs geared towards committing crime. These applications are not only being updated and iterated upon on a near monthly basis, but they have spawned imitation applications that are too numerous to be named here. The success of these darknet applications also continues to inspire black hat hackers to develop new, multi-modal tools geared towards criminal activity beyond the phishing or hacking scams typical of Worm and FraudGPT.

CONCLUSION

3.28 Of the many challenges the dark web presents for governments and public bodies around the globe, there are three worth particular mention here. First, the dark web is predicated on anonymity. This makes it difficult for the authorities to track and apprehend criminals operating on these platforms. Secondly, many dark web marketplaces operate on servers located in countries with lax cybercrime laws, making it difficult for law enforcement agencies to pursue criminals across borders. Finally, the dark web is particularly technically complex; it is extremely challenging for the police and other governmental agencies to infiltrate and monitor these platforms.

65 Mercedes Page, 'Malicious AI arrives on the dark web,' *Australian Strategic Policy Institute* (22 August 2023) < https://netenrich.com/blog/fraudgpt-the-villain-avatar-of-chatgpt>

Chapter 4

AI for crime detection and prevention

4.01 Both the police and government are increasingly leveraging advanced technologies – including AI – to enhance police and governmental efforts to prevent and detect criminal activity. Such is the increase that, in March 2024, the National Police Chiefs' Council (NPCC) announced its first lead for Artificial Intelligence, Temporary Chief Constable Alex Murray.[1] In his new role, Murray will coordinate collaborations with the Office of the Chief Scientific Adviser, academia, industry, and other partners to implement the 'Covenant for Using AI in Policing[2] across the UK[3]. Murray has already stated that he intends to make the preparation of prosecution case files a 'problem of the past' within the next two years; at a panel discussion at the Police Superintendents' Association conference, he announced that trials are already underway to test AI's ability to automate police paperwork[4]. Meanwhile, in April 2024, the College of Policing announced the launch of a new Centre for Police Productivity aimed at using AI and data processing to spot emerging trends and tactics to 'drive efficiency' and 'free up officer time on the frontline[5].' The near-term goal is to have AI undertake tasks that are, typically, 'riddled with error and disappointment': 'through an interaction, AI could write a statement, do a risk assessment, do a crime report, do a handover network which then needs to be signed off by humans who check it is correct. But it can absorb all the digital and written data and create a prosecution file.'[6]

4.02 Given the integral role that AI will shortly occupy in crime detection and prevention across the UK, this chapter will provide an overview of the ways in which AI is already being used to these ends:

1 Predictive policing;

2 Facial recognition; and

3 Criminal investigation/case management.

---

1 'NPCC welcomes first ever lead for Artificial Intelligence (AI),' *NPCC.Police.UK* (28 March 2024).

2 *Covenant for Using Artificial Intelligence (AI) in Policing,* National Police Chiefs' Council (28 September 2023) <https://science.police.uk/delivery/resources/covenant-for-using-artificial-intelligence-ai-in-policing/>

3 'NPCC welcomes first ever lead for Artificial Intelligence (AI),' *NPCC.Police.UK* (28 March 2024).

4 'AI needs to be injected into police force 'like heroin into bloodstream,' says leading officer,' (10 September 2024) *The Independent.co.uk* <https://www.independent.co.uk/news/uk/crime/artificial-intelligence-police-paperwork-andy-marsh-b2610133.html>

5 'Police using data to tackle crime and free up officer time,' *College of Policing.UK* (23 April 2024) <https://www.college.police.uk/article/police-using-data-tackle-crime-and-free-officer-time>

6 'AI needs to be injected into police force 'like heroin into bloodstream,' says leading officer,' (10 September 2024) The Independent.co.uk. <https://www.independent.co.uk/news/uk/crime/artificial-intelligence-police-paperwork-andy-marsh-b2610133.html>

4.03 We will also briefly touch upon:

4 Cybercrime detection;

5 Natural Language Processing (NLP) for threat detection;

6 Automatic number plate recognition (ANPR) and

7 Drone surveillance.

4.04 This list is by no means exhaustive but should give readers a sense of the ways in which AI is expanding upon conventional policing techniques whilst offering the authorities new opportunities and methods for addressing crime.

PREDICTIVE POLICING

4.05 The term 'predictive policing' refers to the use of AI and data analytics to forecast where crimes are likely to happen or to identify individuals who may be/become involved in criminal activities[7]. Broadly, there are two types of predictive policing AI systems: (1) predictive mapping programs; and (2) individual risk assessment programs. Predictive mapping software uses a wide variety of data – including historical crime records, social factors, and environmental conditions – to identify 'hot spots' on a map, thus allowing authorities to allocate resources to high-risk areas (often referred to as 'hotspot policing')[8]. Individual risk assessment systems use similar data but to predict how individual people will behave, including the likelihood of an individual's reoffending or of their becoming a victim of certain crimes[9].

4.06 According to the human rights organisation, Liberty UK, 14 police forces in the UK have already used or intend to use predictive policing in their workflows[10]. Two prime examples of how AI has already been operationalised in UK policing are: (1) the National Data Analytics Solution (NDAS); and (2) Durham's Harm Assessment Risk Tool (HART).

4.07 The NDAS is a project, led by West Midlands Police, that combines AI and machine learning to predict violent crimes like gun or knife attacks[11]. By analysing data from various police databases, the system identifies individuals at high risk of reoffending. NDAS aims to assess and intervene before crimes escalate, potentially involving social services or health workers for support as an alternative to preemptive arrests.

---

7 Jarrod Sadulski, 'Artificial Intelligence in Crime Detection: How It's Useful,' *American Military University* (12 June 2024) <https://www.amu.apus.edu/area-of-study/information-technology/resources/artificial-intelligence-in-crime-detection/>

8 'Predictive Policing,' *Liberty UK* <https://www.libertyhumanrights.org.uk/fundamental/predictive-policing/>

9 'Predictive Policing,' *Liberty UK* <https://www.libertyhumanrights.org.uk/fundamental/predictive-policing/>

10 *Report: Policing by Machine,* Liberty UK (1 February 2019) <https://www.libertyhumanrights.org.uk/issue/policing-by-machine/>, p 45-46

11 Laurence Sherman and Geoffrey Barnes, 'Helping police make custody decisions using artificial intelligence,' in *Research Horizons* (Cambridge University, 26 February 2018) <https://www.cam.ac.uk/research/features/helping-police-make-custody-decisions-using-artificial-intelligence>

4.08 Meanwhile, HART has long been used by Durham Constabulary to predict reoffending. By analysing criminal histories and other variables, HART classifies individuals as low, moderate, or high risk. This tool helps police determine whether to detain suspects or release them on bail. It is part of a broader effort to focus resources on individuals posing significant risks while providing alternatives, like the Checkpoint program, for moderate-risk offenders[12].

FACIAL RECOGNITION

4.09 AI-powered facial recognition systems are already being deployed in public spaces and integrated into CCTV networks in England and Wales. These systems operate by scanning live video feeds or photographs, comparing the facial features against profiles stored in criminal databases, and alerting police where there is a potential match. Though facial recognition software was first trialled in Swansea in 2020[13], the most high-profile instances of its deployment in the UK have all taken place in the last 12–16 months.

4.10 With the rise of AI, the general public has become increasingly concerned with the privacy and racial bias implications of Live Facial Recognition (LFR) AI. LFR is a process in which AI compares live CCTV or other video footage against a predetermined watch-list (eg terrorist suspects, paedophiles in the local area, etc). The algorithm will continuously scrape the feed and compare it to the watchlist to find a possible match that generates an alert.[14] Despite public concerns, the South Wales Police restarted their efforts to use LFR within their area in April 2023[15]. The technology was also used to capture three wanted suspects at a Premier League football match at Emirates Stadium in London in September 2023. Images of thousands of fans were captured by surveillance vans as they made their way into the Arsenal v Tottenham game; these images were cross-referenced against thousands of images of offenders (alleged violent criminals and those subject to football banning orders) stored in a 'watchlist' database in real-time, allowing officers to arrest the individuals before they entered the stadium[16]. A month later, Essex Police announced it had begun trialling LFR in public spaces in Chelmsford and

12 Iryna Mahalias, 'AI adoption in criminal justice – How can industry support the justice system in implementing Artificial Intelligence,' *TechUK – Industry Views* (25 June 2024) <https://www.techuk.org/resource/ai-adoption-in-criminal-justice-how-can-industry-support-the-justice-system-in-implementing-artificial-intelligence.html#:~:text=In%20the%20UK%2C%20AI%20tools,historical%20data%2C%20providing%20appropriate%20measures.>

13 Rachael Burford, 'Wide eye of the law: Facial recognition deployed at Arsenal v Tottenham Premier League clash,' *The Standard* (27 October 2023) <https://www.standard.co.uk/news/london/facial-recognition-met-police-football-arsenal-tottenham-b1116370.html>

14 Tony Mansfield, *Facial Recognition Technology in Law Enforcement: Equitability Study – Final Report* (March 2023) NPL Report MS 43 <https://science.police.uk/site/assets/files/3396/frt-equitability-study_mar2023.pdf> , p 3.

15 'Facial recognition tech: Liberty 'police racism' claim,' *BBC News* (8 April 2023) <https://www.bbc.co.uk/news/uk-wales-65214494>

16 Rachael Burford, 'Wide eye of the law: Facial recognition deployed at Arsenal v Tottenham Premier League clash,' *The Standard* (27 October 2023).<https://www.standard.co.uk/news/london/facial-recognition-met-police-football-arsenal-tottenham-b1116370.html>

Southend[17]. These efforts were publicly supported by the former Policing Minister, Chris Philp, who also actively encouraged all police to operate LFR to 'stay one step ahead of criminals.'[18]

4.11 Another form of widely used facial recognition software is retrospective. Retrospective facial recognition sees AI being used to compare photographs (still images) of faces against an image database. When officers input an image, the AI system generates a candidate list of the records that 'best match' the photograph submitted[19]. The third form of FR is operator-initiated facial recognition: this near-real-time FR sees an officer take a photograph of a suspect via their mobile phone and submit it to an AI system that immediately compares it against an image database.[20]

4.12 Both of these forms of FR are particularly useful for the identification of victims of human trafficking and/or missing persons; the software can cross reference images scraped from the internet, dark web, or CCTV footage with photographs of the trafficking victims or missing individuals and alert the authorities to potential matches.

CRIMINAL INVESTIGATION AND CASE MANAGEMENT

4.13 As previously intimated, AI is already being used to assist law enforcement in managing and organising large amounts of data from investigations, helping them connect dots across different cases more efficiently, and to generate prosecution files. A prime example of how AI is already being tested for case management and triaging for the purposes of resource allocation, is the Control Room AI Assistant,' developed by Untrite AI[21] . Humberside Police ran a three-month long test of the 'Control Room AI Assistant' in early 2024[22]. The software has been specifically designed: (1) to help call handlers capture details given to them by callers both more accurately and more quickly; (2) automatically to recognise key information such as locations or names given during a call to reduce the 'stress on the citizen and operator, by removing the need constantly to repeat key [information] [...] in less-than-ideal background environments or circumstances'; and (3) to assist operators in making more timely and more accurate decisions regarding assigning appropriate policing resources to situations[23].

17 Donna Ferguson and agencies, 'Police urged to double use of facial recognition software,' *The Guardian UK* (29 October 2023) <https://www.theguardian.com/technology/2023/oct/29/uk-police-urged-to-double-use-of-facial-recognition-software>
18 Donna Ferguson and agencies, 'Police urged to double use of facial recognition software,' *The Guardian UK* (29 October 2023) <https://www.theguardian.com/technology/2023/oct/29/uk-police-urged-to-double-use-of-facial-recognition-software>
19 Tony Mansfield, *Facial Recognition Technology in Law Enforcement: Equitability Study – Final Report* (March 2023) NPL Report MS 43 <https://science.police.uk/site/assets/files/3396/frt-equitability-study_mar2023.pdf> , p. 2
20 Tony Mansfield, *Facial Recognition Technology in Law Enforcement: Equitability Study – Final Report* (March 2023) NPL Report MS 43 <https://science.police.uk/site/assets/files/3396/frt-equitability-study_mar2023.pdf> , p. 3
21 *Untrite AI* <https://untrite.com/product/untrite-thrive/>
22 Jane Wakefield, 'Should AI play an ever-growing role in tackling crime?' *BBC News* (26 January 2024) <https://www.bbc.com/news/business-68067081>
23 *Untrite AI* <https://untrite.com/product/untrite-thrive/>

4.14 During the three-month trial period, the AI Assistant was used to respond to fictitious domestic abuse 999 emergency calls. A call would come in from a 'victim' and the AI Assistant would transcribe the call for the human police officer, linking directly into UK police databases and automatically retrieving any relevant documentation – eg her husband's date of birth and a special alert flagging that he has a firearm certificate[24]. The system was trained on two years of historic data related to domestic abuse calls, all from Humberside's area. When interviewed about the trials, Untrite's CEO and co-founder, Kamila Hankiewicz, explained that the system is designed to produce a triaging score – low, medium, or high – where a high score means an officer must be at the scene within 5–10 minutes[25]. Overall, the company claims the technology will save emergency services nearly ⅓ of their time. They are already in talks with a number of UK-based police and emergency services who are interested in deploying the tech in live environments.

4.15 Meanwhile, Bedfordshire Police have been using an AI system called DocDefender[26] to redact personal and sensitive data from case files before they are sent to the Crown Prosecution Service (CPS)[27]. The AI system can remove all the data that is not relevant to the investigation within 10–15 minutes; the same task would have taken a team of officers several days to complete manually translating into a saving of approximately 9,525 hours of police and staff time per year[28]. According to the BBC report, the system searches for categories of information that are specifically selected by the officer[29]. Data that is inputted into the system is only stored for up to 12 hours.

4.16 Beyond case management, AI can also help analyse forensic evidence, such as fingerprints, DNA, or ballistics, more quickly and accurately. Advanced algorithms improve image and video analysis, which helps in reviewing CCTV footage or identifying crucial details at crime scenes. For example, it can monitor CCTV footage for abnormal behaviour patterns, such as loitering in high-security areas or suspicious body language. This can then trigger alerts for potential criminal activities or preemptive security measures in public spaces, like airports or train stations.

4.17 Avon and Somerset Police are currently trialling AI systems to try to identify potential leads in cold cases[30]. The software, Soze, was developed in Australia and can perform a number of functions simultaneously, including: analysing video footage and images (FR); trawling

---

24 Jane Wakefield, 'Should AI play an ever-growing role in tackling crime?' *BBC News* (26 January 2024) <https://www.bbc.com/news/business-68067081>

25 Jane Wakefield, 'Should AI play an ever-growing role in tackling crime?' *BBC News* (26 January 2024) <https://www.bbc.com/news/business-68067081>

26 *DocDefender* <https://docdefender.net/>

27 Janine Machin, 'Bedfordshire Police use AI to save hours on admin duties,' *BBC News* (14 December 2023) <https://www.bbc.co.uk/news/uk-england-cambridgeshire-67680698>

28 'Auto-redaction of text for transfer to the Crown Prosecution Service,' *College of Policing* (12 December 2023) <https://www.college.police.uk/support-forces/practices/auto-redaction-text-transfer-crown-prosecution-service>

29 Janine Machin, 'Bedfordshire Police use AI to save hours on admin duties,' *BBC News* (14 December 2023) <https://www.bbc.co.uk/news/uk-england-cambridgeshire-67680698>

30 Henry Vaughan, 'AI tool that can do '81 years of detective work in 30 hours' trialled by police,' (24 September 2024) *Sky News* < https://news.sky.com/story/ai-tool-that-can-do-81-years-of-detective-work-in-30-hours-trialled-by-police-13220891>

through financial transactions and social media content automatically to construct timelines of events; reconstructing conversations from texts, phone calls, and emails; providing translated results from foreign language content and documents; and providing association analysis across data-types and documents[31]. Early evaluations of the software's performance have shown that it can review evidential material from 27 complex criminal cases in just 30 hours; this same task would have taken a team of human police officers approximately 81 years to complete.[32] In an interview with Sky News in September 2024, the chair of the National Police Chiefs' Council, Gavin Stephens, revealed that Soze is just one of many tools they plan to roll out across the UK.[33] The 64 different AI systems being explored would save approximately 15 million hours of police officers' time, in turn saving the state approximately £350 million in costs.[34]

4.18 Cybercrime detection

AI systems are used proactively to identify unusual patterns in financial transactions that may indicate fraud, money laundering, or identity theft. Algorithms can detect anomalies in banking, online payment systems, and insurance claims: genAI/ ML analyses customer behaviour, account activity, and credit card transaction patterns so it can flag unusual patterns as they occur (eg multiple transactions from different locations or sudden changes in spending patterns). AI systems can also uncover fraudulent networks by analysing the relationships between entities and flagging unusual connections. AI is also frequently used to continuously up-date detection models and frameworks so that they remain abreast of emerging fraud patterns and emerging tactics.

4.19 As discussed at length in the previous chapter, AI also helps detect and prevent phishing attacks by analysing email content, flagging malicious messages, and tracking suspicious online behaviour. AI can warn users about suspicious links and automatically report fraudulent accounts to platform owners.

4.20 Natural Language Processing (NLP) for threat detection

AI is a powerful tool for social media monitoring: AI tools using NLP can analyse large volumes of online content, such as social media posts, forums, and chat rooms, to detect potential threats. This can include monitoring for extremist rhetoric, hate speech, paedophilia/ sex trafficking, or indicators of planned criminal activity. It is a particularly effective tool for tackling child trafficking as traffickers commonly post advertisements of trafficked victims; in using NLP to

---

31 *Soze – Police and Intelligence Investigation integrated AI Solution (Azure),* Gov.UK Digital Marketplace <https://www.applytosupply.digitalmarketplace.service.gov.uk/g-cloud/services/946905927824217>

32 Henry Vaughan, 'AI tool that can do '81 years of detective work in 30 hours' trialled by police,' (24 September 2024) *Sky News* < https://news.sky.com/story/ai-tool-that-can-do-81-years-of-detective-work-in-30-hours-trialled-by-police-13220891>

33 Henry Vaughan, 'AI tool that can do '81 years of detective work in 30 hours' trialled by police,' (24 September 2024) *Sky News* < https://news.sky.com/story/ai-tool-that-can-do-81-years-of-detective-work-in-30-hours-trialled-by-police-13220891>

34 Henry Vaughan, 'AI tool that can do '81 years of detective work in 30 hours' trialled by police,' (24 September 2024) *Sky News* < https://news.sky.com/story/ai-tool-that-can-do-81-years-of-detective-work-in-30-hours-trialled-by-police-13220891>

scan for keywords or images associated with the trading of victims, AI can detect when and where a child is being sold[35].

4.21 NLP is also routinely used in counter-terrorism. The UK's counter-terrorism units have used AI to flag potential terrorist communications and monitor radicalisation trends online.

Finally, as previously discussed, NLP is used to access websites' legitimacy – it reviews user content, reviews, and transaction history to protect e-commerce customers from fraudulent websites[36].

4.22 Automatic Number Plate Recognition (ANPR)

Automatic Number Plate Recognition (ANPR) systems help law enforcement track vehicles involved in criminal activities, such as car theft, smuggling, or getaway cars used in crimes.[37] ANPR cameras are widely deployed on UK roads; the technology instantly checks a vehicle's registration number against police records of 'vehicles of interest'. When a vehicle is flagged, the police are mobilised to stop the vehicle and – if necessary – make an arrest.

4.23 Drones: surveillance and military deployment

In a public statement issued on 16 March 2021, the Mayor of London, Sadiq Khan (now Sir), confirmed that drones are used 'for coverage of crime scenes, providing aerial support for pre-planned operations, surveying premises, and providing life footage of operational deployments to assist command decision making and therefore support a wider policing plan[38].' Furthermore, Kent Police has confirmed it began using drones to support its policing activities in 2017, including for: searches for suspects, vulnerable missing people, stolen property, and stolen vehicles; getting aerial imagery of crime scenes and serious road traffic accidents; getting aerial images of sensitive sites[39]. The Metropolitan and Kent Police forces are not unique, however. In 2020, 40 UK police forces confirmed they were using drones[40]. For example, in 2019, Police Scotland unveiled a drone system for helping in police searches for missing and/or vulnerable people[41]. Meanwhile, in 2021, the Guardian reported that UK police forces have been using drone technology to monitor political protests since 2020[42].

35
36 Gemma Marin, 'Machine Learning and AI in Fraud detection,' (May 2024) *Experian.co.uk* <https://www.experian.co.uk/blogs/latest-thinking/guide/machine-learning-ai-fraud-detection/>
37 Automatic Number Plat Recognition (ANPR),' *The Metropolitan Police* <https://www.met.police.uk/advice/advice-and-information/rs/road-safety/automatic-number-plate-recognition-anpr/>
38 'Use of Drones in policing,' (November 2022) *The Metropolitan Police* <https://www.met.police.uk/foi-ai/metropolitan-police/d/november-2022/use-of-drones-in-policing/>
39 'Unmanned aerial vehicles (drones),' *Kent Police* <https://www.kent.police.uk/foi-ai/kent-police/who-we-are/unmanned-aerial-vehicle-drones/>
40 Use of Drones in policing,' (November 2022) *The Metropolitan Police* <https://www.met.police.uk/foi-ai/metropolitan-police/d/november-2022/use-of-drones-in-policing/>
41 Ken Macdonald, 'Police to use AI recognition drones to help find the missing,' (4 November 2019) *BBC News* <https://www.bbc.co.uk/news/uk-scotland-50262650>
42 Vikram Dodd, 'Drones used by police to monitor political protests in England,' *The Guardian UK* <https://www.theguardian.com/uk-news/2021/feb/14/drones-police-england-monitor-political-protests-blm-extinction-rebellion>

4.24 It should also be noted that in August 2024, the UK Ministry of Defence, the US Department of Defense and the Australian Department of Defence piloted AI-enabled uncrewed aerial vehicles (drones). The drones are the first use of 'autonomy and AI sensing systems in real-time military environments'; they allow a remote human operative to identify enemy targets and destroy in a fraction of the time[43].

CONCLUSION: THE BIAS PROBLEM

4.25 Because algorithms analyse past data to provide objective insights, AI in/for policing raises a number of challenges regarding fairness and transparency. Specifically, numerous studies have demonstrated that AI systems inherit biases from the data they are trained on, leading to outputs that unfairly target minority groups. For example, the UK's National Physical Laboratory (NPL), Britain's official measurement standards body, undertook independent testing of LFR and retrospective AI systems in 2023, with a particular focus on the software already being employed by the Metropolitan police and the South Wales police. Their equitability study found that, while LFR systems had become increasingly more accurate in recent years, they are still likely to provide a 'statistically significant' number of false-positive identifications for black individuals compared to white or Asian.[44] Similarly, studies of mass-deployment of AI facial recognition systems in large cities in the US have revealed that the technology fails to accurately identify black faces[45]. Albert Cahn, director of the Surveillance Technology Oversight Project (Stop), confirms that facial recognition – particularly, LFR – discriminates against black, Asian, and Latino individuals, in particular, Black women[46].

4.26 These concerns, coupled with the fact that it is sometimes difficult to determine accountability when AI systems make mistakes or when their decisions impact individuals' lives, have led human rights groups such as Liberty UK, to petition for the ban of AI in public spaces[47]. Given the enthusiasm with which the technology is being adopted by emergency services across Britain, it is unlikely these efforts will be more than partially successful.

---

43 Defense Science and Technology Laboratory, 'AUKUS takes another step forward with real-time AI trials,' (9 August 2024) <https://www.gov.uk/government/news/aukus-takes-another-step-forward-with-real-time-ai-trials>

44 Tony Mansfield, *Facial Recognition Technology in Law Enforcement: Equitability Study – Final Report* (March 2023) NPL Report MS 43 <https://science.police.uk/site/assets/files/3396/frt-equitability-study_mar2023.pdf> , p. 3

45 Thaddeus L. Johnson and Natasha N. Johnson, 'Police Facial Recognition Technology Can't Tell Black People Apart,' (18 May 2023) *The Scientific American* <https://www.scientificamerican.com/article/police-facial-recognition-technology-cant-tell-black-people-apart/>

46 Jane Wakefield, 'Should AI play an ever-growing role in tackling crime?' *BBC News* (26 January 2024) <https://www.bbc.com/news/business-68067081>

47 'Liberty Report Exposes Police Forces' Use of Discriminatory Data to Predict Crime,' (4 February 2019) *Liberty UK* <https://www.libertyhumanrights.org.uk/issue/liberty-report-exposes-police-forces-use-of-discriminatory-data-to-predict-crime/>

Part 3: AI in Legal Practice

Chapter 5

AI in your legal practice: the preliminaries

5.01 When deciding whether and how to take the plunge into using AI in your legal practice, there are some fundamental considerations that first need to be confronted. In this chapter, we break these down into three stages:

1 Reading the (data and ownership) fine print;

2 Choosing your AI platform;

3 Signing up for a (paid) account.

5.02 We will provide a step-by-step guide for how to complete each stage, while also providing questions we advise you ask yourselves, your chambers or your employers, and your clients before, during, and after employing AI in your practice. By keeping these data privacy and data protection questions in mind at all times, not only will you ensure that you use AI in accordance with existing best practice in your places of employment but also that you use this technology in your practice in accordance with the Code(s) of Conduct developed by legal regulators in the UK.

STAGE 1: READING THE (DATA AND OWNERSHIP) FINE PRINT

5.03 As stated in the introduction, two of the main generative AI (now, multimodal) models available to the general public today are: (1) Open AI's ChatGPT; and (2) Google's Gemini. Though the two genAI models largely perform the same functions, their terms and conditions differ in a number of key areas. Among the most important for legal practitioners is that each company has a different stance on data ownership and usage: who has the rights to the data that is fed into a model or that is generated by the model in response to a prompt; and whether the provider has the right to use or share the data generated by model with other users?

5.04 Both AI models typically retain user data for a certain period to improve their performance and for legal compliance purposes. However, they may offer users options to delete their data or request a copy. Similarly, both may share data with third-party service providers for purposes such as infrastructure, analytics, or legal compliance. They typically have measures in place to protect data privacy and prevent unauthorised access. Users of these (and most other) models – particularly if based in the EU and/or UK – generally have the right to access, correct, or delete their personal data under the DPA and UK GDPR. They likely also have the option to opt out of certain data collection or usage practices.

5.05 In terms of specific differences between Gemini and Chat-GPT, what follows is a (non-exhaustive) comparison of their data ownership policies.

OpenAI

5.06 ChatGPT is owned by the US company, OpenAI. The model's Terms of Service for the EU and UK[1] state that users retain ownership of all data they feed into the model via their prompts as well as the data output the model generates in response to their queries. However, OpenAI clearly states that they will use users' content to 'provide, maintain, develop, and improve' ChatGPT as well as to enforce their terms of use, policies, to keep their users safe, and to comply with applicable laws. However, since their launch, they have introduced additional measures to protect user privacy, such as allowing users to (somewhat) opt out of having their data used for model training[2]. ChatGPT's data terms and conditions dictate that avoiding ChatGPT for aspects of legal practice involving sensitive data is advisable; see 5.11 below.

5.07 As well as data ownership, the company specifically addresses ChatGPT's (in)accuracy in their Terms of Use; they warn that ML is probabilistic meaning the model can generate answers that do not accurately reflect facts or reality. The terms state that, when an individual uses their models, they must understand and agree that they should not rely on ChatGPT as the sole source of factual information or as a substitute for professional advice. They stress human review to check for accuracy and appropriateness before using or sharing output generated by the model. It is a further term of use that output will not be used in any manner that could have a legal or material impact on a person.

5.08 The company also has a Europe privacy policy that is worth looking at[3]. The policy applies to all those in the European Economic Area (EEA), the UK or Switzerland. It does not, however, apply to those who use OpenAI Enterprise, the business offering of the FM (described below). For those living in the UK, OpenAI OpCo LLC, in San Francisco is the data controller and is responsible for processing all users' personal data. Such data includes data that users input into their accounts – name, contact and payment information – as well as data that is collected automatically: your IP address when using OpenAI, how you interact with ChatGPT (the type of content you view and/or engage with), the features you use and actions you take, type of computer or mobile device you are using, and your computer connection. They also receive data from third-parties, including information that is publicly available on the

1 Europe Terms of Use (14 November 2023) *OpenAI* <https://openai.com/policies/eu-terms-of-use/>
2 'How your data is used to improve model performance,' (September 2024) OpenAI Help Center <https://help.openai.com/en/articles/5722486-how-your-data-is-used-to-improve-model-performance>
3 'Europe Privacy Policy', (15 February 2024) OpenAI.com <https://openai.com/policies/privacy-policy/>

internet, security information to protect against abuse, and information from marketing vendors who identify potential customers of OpenAI's business. This information is used to provide, maintain, improve, and develop OpenAI's services, to conduct research, to prevent fraud and criminal activity, as well as to comply with the company's legal obligations to protect the right to privacy, safety, and IP of users and third-parties. There is a breakdown of the legal bases the company uses for processing Personal Data in section 8, 'Legal bases for processing,' of the Privacy Policy.

5.09 Once collected and/or shared with OpenAI, the company may disclose your Personal Data:

1 Vendors and service providers: third parties that host their services, customer service vendors, web analytics services, or content delivery services may all be made privy to your private data;

2 Business transfers: in the event OpenAI goes bankrupt, goes into receivership, or otherwise undergoes a reorganisation, all personal data will be disclosed during the diligence process with both counterparties and those assisting in the process;

3 Government Authorities or Other Third Parties: private data may be shared with government authorities, industry 'peers' or other third parties in compliance with their legal obligations, to protect OpenAI's rights and property, or in the event a user violates OpenAI's policies or terms. They will also share private data to protect themselves from liability and to detect illegal or fraudulent activity;

4 Affiliates: they may disclose private data to entities that control, are controlled by, or are under common control with OpenAI;

5 Other Users: certain features on ChatGPT allow you to share or display information to other users (eg 'share' links or sending information to third-party apps).

5.10 OpenAI's privacy policy states it will only retain personal data for as long as they need to provide their service and for other legitimate business purposes. A user's settings will also impact the duration of data retention. The policy lists the statutory rights user's have in relation to their data, all of which mirror the data protections codified in the DPA 2018 and UK GDPR: data access, data erasure, data portability, right to object (to withdraw consent) to process data for marketing or for legitimate business interests, right to complain to OpenAI and/or to the local data protection authority. However, these rights may be limited if, for example, a user asks OpenAI to delete information they are required to retain by law or if they 'have compelling legitimate interests to keep [it].' Worryingly, there is no sense of what those interests may be. Finally, OpenAI may transfer personal data outside the EEA, Switzerland or the UK when, for example, third party affiliates are located in third countries. This occurs regardless of whether the third countries offer the same level of data protection as the user's home country or not. However, OpenAI states they transfer all data pursuant to the European Commission's adequacy decisions on certain countries or, if not applicable, in compliance with Standard Contractual Clauses as approved by the EC (and any applicable country addenda). Moreover, in using ChatGPT in the

UK, users understand and acknowledge that personal data will be processed and stored in OpenAI servers in the US.

5.11 Finally, it is important to note that OpenAI uses human reviewers, to monitor and investigate potential security and safety breaches as well as to improve/fine-tune their services by generating content. There is not much information available about how human reviewers work or what exactly they work on; the company has merely stated that ChatGPT is developed using: (1) information publicly available on the internet; (2) information they license from third parties; (3) information that users provide; and (4) information that their human trainers provide. Given this, it is not advisable to share any sensitive content with the free version of ChatGPT as there is no guarantee the information will not be used for training or as part of an unspecified human review process[4].

Google

5.12 Google's genAI model is known as Gemini (formerly Bard). As with all Google products its use of data aligns with the company's broader privacy policy[5]. The company has also created a Gemini-specific privacy notice[6] to explain to users what data is collected, how it is used, and what users' rights are relative to that data. In the section that follows, we will break down this privacy notice as it applies to users in the UK.

5.13 When you are using Gemini as a free user, Google collects your conversations, your location, your feedback on Gemini (if given), and your usage information. According to the general privacy policy, how much or what data Google collects depends on whether or not you are signed into a Google account when using their services (including Gemini)[7]. If you are not signed in, they store information related to your activity using unique identifiers that can be used to identify your browser, app, or device. This allows the company to maintain user preferences across browsing sessions, remember your language preferences, and to show you search results most relevant to you based on your activity. When you use Google services (including Gemini) while signed in to your Google account, they also collect any personal information you enter and store it with your account; this personal information includes your billing information, name, email address, or other data that can be reasonably linked to this information.

5.14 The Gemini-specific privacy notice states that Gemini collects your conversations with the AI model, related product usage information (devise used, language preference etc), info

4 'How should AI systems behave, and who should decide?' (16 February 2023) *OpenAI* <https://openai.com/index/how-should-ai-systems-behave/>
5 'Google Privacy & Terms,' *Google.com* <https://policies.google.com/privacy#infocollect>
6 'Gemini Apps Privacy Notice,' *Google.com* <https://support.google.com/gemini/answer/13594961?hl=en-GB#privacy_notice>
7 'Information that Google Collects – Privacy Policy, *Google.com* <https://policies.google.com/privacy#infocollect>

about your location (eg IP address), and your feedback (if given)[8]. Google uses this data to provide, improve and develop Gemini and other Google products/ services, as well as other machine learning technologies, including business/enterprise products such as Google Cloud. Google does not use this information to 'serve' you with advertisements; it does not sell this information to third parties.

5.15 Unlike ChatGPT, Gemini gives free users the option of turning off their Gemini activity[9]. If you leave the 'Saving activity' feature on, Google will store your prompts and resulting conversations with Gemini for 18 months. After 18 months, this data will be automatically deleted unless you opt to turn off auto-delete or choose to manually delete your data (possible at any time). This being said, you can also change your Gemini settings to only save data for 3 to 36 months via your Gemini activity settings. If you switch your Activity setting off, your chats with Gemini are only saved for 72 hours before they are automatically deleted; the data stored during this 72-hour period is used to provide the Gemini service, maintain safety and security on the service, and to process any feedback users choose to provide Google. Information about your location – the general area of your device when using the service, IP address, or work/ home addresses in your Google Account – are also stored with your Gemini activity. The default settings for Gemini are active (unless you change them or opt-out) if the user is 18 or older; minors are required to turn My Activity features on manually. Finally, all users also have the option of adding extra security to their chat history with Gemini by turning on extra verification. With this featured turned on, Google will, 'make sure that it is really you' before you can access your full history with Gemini on My Activity[10]. This is particularly useful if you are using Gemini across multiple or shared devices.

5.16 It is very important to note that Google uses human reviewers to improve the free Google AI services. Human reviewers read, annotate, and otherwise process information from chats with Gemini to improve Google's machine learning models. The company takes a number of steps to protect users' privacy including anonymising conversations and disconnecting them from your Google Account etc. before passing them along to human reviewers. It is crucial, however, not to enter confidential information into Gemini or otherwise feed the genAI model data you would not want a human reviewer to see or Google to use to improve their products, services, or ML technologies.[11] If your chats with Gemini are reviewed by a human reviewer, you will not be able to delete them: even if you delete your data on your My Activity page, the review and annotations (including relevant data) are kept separately and are not connected to your Google Account. These are kept for up to three years. If you turn off your Gemini activity, your data settings on other Google services will not change; your location history on Google Maps or Web Activity

8 'What data is collected and how it's used,' *Gemini Apps Help* (updated 24 September 2024) <https://support.google.com/gemini/answer/13594961?hl=en-GB#privacy_notice>

9 *Your Gemini Apps activity* <https://myactivity.google.com/product/gemini?pli=1>

10 *Your Gemini Apps activity* <https://myactivity.google.com/product/gemini?pli=1>

11 'How human reviewers improve Google AI,' *Gemini Apps Help* <https://support.google.com/gemini/answer/13594961?hl=en-GB#privacy_notice>

on Google search will continue saving unless you adjust those default settings on your Google account.[12] **To prevent your chats from being reviewed by humans, turn off Gemini Apps Activity.** In any event, information from your Gmail or your Google Drive is not reviewed or otherwise used to improve Gemini Apps. Therefore, as with ChatGPT, Google AI's free service should not be used for aspects of legal practice involving sensitive data.

5.17 As a free user, you can request that your content be removed under Google's policies, DPA/UK GDPR, or local law, as applicable[13]. Under the DPA and UK GDPR, you can also export your data to another service provider or to back it up in your cloud/ on your personal device[14]. Like OpenAI, Google is very clear that Gemini may sometimes provide inaccurate or inappropriate responses to prompts. As a result, users should not rely on responses from Gemini, particularly for medical, legal, financial or other professional advice. Under the DPA and UK GDPR, you have the right to ask Google to remove inaccurate personal data pertaining to you.

5.18 Like OpenAI, Google also provide information to third parties with legitimate interests, albeit with safeguards in place to protect users' privacy. 'Legitimate interests' includes processing personal data for:

- Providing, maintaining and improving Google services and Gemini's performance (fine-tuning the AI model and improving Gemini's responses in terms of accuracy and safety);
- Developing new products and features (R&D) such as improving how requests are routed to new Large Language Models (LLMs) best suited to responding to the query or training models to handle new requests;
- Understanding users' needs to improve services (eg generating metrics);
- Customising services to specific users to provide them with a better experience (eg using past conversations to provide a more relevant answer to a user's query);
- Detecting, preventing, and responding to fraud, abuse, security risks and technical issues that could negatively impact Google, other users, or the general public;
- Enforcing legal claims, including the investigation of potential violations of applicable terms of service (eg reviewing suspicious activity);
- Processing requests from commercial partners (eg requests from developers and IP rights holders to remove content);
- Meeting legal process or enforceable governmental request (eg request for information from a government authority).

12 'How Gemini Apps activity works with other services and settings,' *Gemini Apps Help* <https://support.google.com/gemini/answer/13594961?hl=en-GB#other_services_and_settings>
13 'Report content for legal reasons,' *Google.com* <https://support.google.com/legal/answer/3110420?visit_id=638650959149510941-245561419&p=gemini_pntos_removal_request&rd=1>
14 *Google Takeout* <https://takeout.google.com/?pli=1>

Enterprise models

5.19 It is important to note that each company has different policies for the paid, business (or enterprise) versions of their genAI models as opposed to their free, publicly available versions.

5.20 OpenAI launched its ChatGPT Enterprise in October 2023 to offer businesses and developers increased security and privacy, longer context windows for submitting longer prompts, advanced data analysis, and a number of other features[15]. The enhanced privacy and data ownership conditions include, importantly, that OpenAI does not use data from the commercial versions of ChatGPT – ChatGPT Team, ChatGPT Enterprise, or their API Platform (after March 2023) – to train their models *unless you explicitly opt-in to share your data with them*[16]. They also do not scrape metadata or otherwise allow their genAI models to learn from users' interactions with their enterprise models. This is because ChatGPT Enterprise messages are encrypted – both when being sent from/to the genAI model and when 'at rest'. Users of ChatGPT Enterprise also control how long their data is retained for by the AI provider[17], a feature that is particularly useful given DPA/UK GDPR obligations regarding only retaining the minimal amount of data for as long as strictly necessary. Finally, users of the Enterprise versions retain complete ownership of any material input into the genAI model as part of their prompts (eg documents, images, etc); they also retain all rights to the outputs they rightfully receive from ChatGPT Enterprise (to the extent permitted by law)[18].

5.21 This being said, OpenAI retains thc right to inputs and outputs necessary to provide users with their services, comply with local laws, and to enforce safety and security policies as well as their terms of use. Any conversations with ChatGPT Enterprise that you delete will be completely wiped from OpenAI's systems after 30 days.Moreover, any business data submitted to ChatGPT Enterprise may be run through content classifier software and other (unspecified) safety tools to ensure OpenAI's services are being used in line with their terms of use. Though they emphasise that the classifiers operate on metadata only (IP addresses, timestamps, geolocations etc.), they do subject business data (the actual content) to human review when deemed necessary[19]. Like Google, OpenAI uses human reviewers however, in the case of ChatGPT Enterprise, reviewers will only ever be allowed access conversations for the purposes of resolving incidents, recovering end user conversations (only with your explicit permission), and when required to do so by law[20].

15 'Introducing ChatGPT Enterprise,' (28 August 2023) *OpenAI.com* <https://openai.com/index/introducing-chatgpt-enterprise/>
16 'Enterprise Privacy at OpenAI,' *OpenAI.com* <https://openai.com/enterprise-privacy/>
17 'Enterprise Privacy at OpenAI,' *OpenAI.com* <https://openai.com/enterprise-privacy/>
18 'Enterprise Privacy at OpenAI,' *OpenAI.com* <https://openai.com/enterprise-privacy/>
19 'Enterprise Privacy at OpenAI,' *OpenAI.com* <https://openai.com/enterprise-privacy/>
20 'Enterprise Privacy at OpenAI,' *OpenAI.com* <https://openai.com/enterprise-privacy/>

5.22 As a final note, UK and EU Users of ChatGPT Enterprise will have to complete a DPA form to execute a Data Protection Addendum[21] (DPA) with OpenAI. Said DPA will allow all Enterprise customers to use the model in compliance with GDPR and other local privacy laws.

5.23 Google also provides users with the option of using a paid-for, commercial version of Gemini. Users must first,register for a qualifying Google Workspace licence (described in further detail below)[22]. This grants their account, their interactions with Gemini, and the data they store in their Google Drive enterprise-level protections: neither chats with Gemini nor uploaded files used in prompts will ever be reviewed by human reviewers or otherwise used to train Google's genAI models[23]. Similarly, the history of interactions you have with Gemini will never be shared outside your organisation. Your organisation's existing controls and data policies will also be automatically applied to your Gemini activity – including UK specific data protections and organisation specific Data Loss Prevention measures.[24] As with the free version of Gemini, conversations with the genAI models are also *not* used for advertising purposes[25].

5.24 For those with some coding knowledge or interest in Python, Google has also developed AI Studio, a paid version of Gemini that allows you to combine prompts (instructions) with examples to show Gemini the kind of response (output) you want[26]. Users can choose whether to use structured prompts or to fine-tune the model, depending on what their needs and level of technical expertise are. Structure prompting is a technique whereby the user provides the genAI model a set of example prompts and responses; it is particularly useful when you want the genAI model to stick to a certain format or to mimic a tone/ particular style[27]. Fine tuning a model is a more advanced technique that allows a user to improve a model's responses to specific prompts by providing it with an example set[28]. By fine-tuning, you are building a custom version of Gemini that suits your specific needs (style, tone, format etc) when it comes to a particular prompt (eg draft a case summary from the following facts and evidence). Because you are feeding the model an example set rather than just a few select examples of the response you are looking for, results tend to be more tailored.

21 *Data Processing Addendum* <https://ironcladapp.com/public-launch/63ffefa2bed6885f4536d0fe>

22 Gemini for Workspace FAQ, *Google Workspace Admin Help* <https://support.google.com/a/answer/14130944#zippy=%2Cwhat-if-i-dont-have-google-workspace-today-what-if-i-dont-have-the-right-edition%2Chow-does-gemini-protect-my-data%2Cwho--can-use-the-gemini-app>

23 'How we're protecting your Google Workspace data in the era of generative AI,' (11 August 2023) *Google Workspace* <https://workspace.google.com/blog/identity-and-security/protecting-your-data-era-generative-ai>

24 Gemini for Workspace FAQ, *Google Workspace Admin Help* <https://support.google.com/a/answer/14130944#zippy=%2Cwhat-if-i-dont-have-google-workspace-today-what-if-i-dont-have-the-right-edition%2Chow-does-gemini-protect-my-data%2Cwho--can-use-the-gemini-app>

25 'Enterprise-grade Gemini is now available for teams of all sizes with Google Workspace,' (21 February 2024) *Google Workspace* <https://workspace.google.com/blog/product-announcements/gemini-for-google-workspace>

26 'Google AI Studio quickstart', *Google AI for Developers* <https://ai.google.dev/gemini-api/docs/ai-studio-quickstart#:~:text=Structured%20prompts%20in%20Google%20AI,telling%20it%20what%20to%20do.>

27 'Google AI Studio quickstart', *Google AI for Developers* <https://ai.google.dev/gemini-api/docs/ai-studio-quickstart#:~:text=Structured%20prompts%20in%20Google%20AI,telling%20it%20what%20to%20do.>

28 'Fine-tuning with the Gemini API,' *Google AI for Developers* <https://ai.google.dev/gemini-api/docs/model-tuning?_gl=1*te419c*_up*MQ..*_ga*MTgyMjMwMDQwMy4xNzMwMTA1MjEx*_ga_P1DBVKWT6V*MTczMDEwNTIxMC4xLjAuMTczMDEwNTIxMC4wLjAuNzM1MDgyMjc.>

STAGE 2: CHOOSING YOUR AI PLATFORM

5.25 There are a number of other factors to consider when choosing which genAI model best suits your needs:

1 Specific Terms and Conditions: As already mentioned, each platform has unique terms and conditions regarding data privacy that may (not) comply with your employer's or chambers' data privacy policies, or your professional obligations to your clients, so it is crucial to read the individual policies carefully.

2 Updates and Changes: Privacy policies can change over time, so it is important to check for any updates or modifications on a regular basis (eg once a fiscal quarter). We also recommend setting up an email alert so you are immediately notified when your chosen GenAI provider announces changes to their privacy or data ownership T&Cs.

3 Regulatory Compliance: These platforms are likely to become subject to new and emerging AI legislation such as the EU AI Act and the Labour government's proposed AI Bill. It is, therefore, key to understand if and how your obligations change as these new legal obligations come into effect.

4 Law firm/chambers' requirements/professional obligations: it is important to discuss data privacy and data protection policies with your chambers'/employer's IT and compliance departments and to consider your professional code of conduct to determine:

    a What cloud service they will/will not allow you to use when storing private and confidential information (eg iCloud, Google Drive, Amazon WS, etc.);

    b How long you are allowed to store private and confidential data before you are required to delete it under your/your chambers'/employers' standard terms and conditions when contracting with clients;

    c What levels of encryption or log-in protections you are required to have on clients' information (two-step authentication, end-to-end encryption, etc)

    d What disclosures must you make to clients (if any) when using AI to process, analyse, or summarise their information.

5.26 It is important to choose what AI model to use in your practice based on the data and data ownership terms outlined in section 1 and the additional considerations above. For the most accurate and up-to-date information, please visit the official privacy policies of ChatGPT, Gemini, and competing genAI models (eg Llama, Claude).

5.27 We elected to use Google Gemini for the examples in this book for the following reasons:

1 At the time of writing, Google was more transparent than OpenAI about how it used (or did not use) client's data;

2 At the time of writing, Google had confirmed that human reviewers had no access to enterprise client's data;

3 Google Drive was a cloud service that both co-authors already used and, therefore, were familiar with;

4 OpenAI requires UK/EU users to fill out an additional Data Protection Addendum to ensure compliance with the (UK)GDPR and other data protections. Google, however, automatically makes user accounts EU/UK DPA compliant when an account is registered in these geo-locations.

STAGE 3: SIGNING UP FOR YOUR (PAID) ACCOUNT

5.28 For the purposes of this section, we will provide you with a step-by-step guide to setting up: 1. your Google Workspace Enterprise account for Google Gemini; and 2. A Google AI Studio API.

5.29 Whether you want to use Google AI Studio or Gemini for Google Workspace, you need to create a Workspace account. Google Workspace provides a number of enterprise versions for users to choose from, depending on their AI usage. Gemini Business is recommended for those who use AI at light to moderate levels; the accounts are cheaper but are subject to usage limits in terms of how many prompts users can ask Gemini per month. Gemini Enterprise (formerly Duet AI for Workspace Enterprise) is recommended for those who use generative AI heavily though it does come at a higher price point ($30 USD per month, with an annual commitment)[29]. It is important to note that uploading large files for AI to analyse or summarise is considered 'heavy' usage meaning a Gemini Enterprise account may be most useful for legal practitioners.

5.30 Steps for creating a Google Workspace account:

1 Go to workspace.google.com

2 Click on 'Get Started Now'

3 Create an account by following the directions on the 'Let's get started' page

4 Choose a way to set up your account

You can choose between one of three options, depending on your needs/ your organisation's needs. If you wish to create a workspace for up to 300 employees, click on 'Get a new custom domain'. If you already have a domain and wish to create a workspace for up to 300 employees, click on 'set up using your existing domain.' You cannot use Gemini Enterprise with the third option (a single-person business account). A domain is the address that comes

29 Gemini for Workspace, *Gemini Workspace Admin Help* <https://support.google.com/a/answer/13623623?co=DASHER._Family%3DBusiness-Enterprise&oco=0#get_gemini>

after the @ in an email address. For example, if your email address was tonyf@chambers.com, then chambers.com would be the domain.

For this example, we will set up a new custom domain: aicrimbook.com. Choose a domain name that is not in use by anyone else. This will be the gmail account associated with your Gemini activity so pick a domain name that is suitable for your needs.

It will cost £10 to buy your unique domain name, if you do not already have one. This is an annual cost that will be processed by Google through Squarespace on your behalf.

5 Create your username and password.

This is what will be in front of the @ in your email address. In this example, our username will be 'author' which means that our workspace email will be: author@aicrimbook.com.

6 Sign up for the Business Standard plan.

7 Add your credit or debit card

A workspace account costs £12 monthly approx (price as of October 2024). Payments start after your initial 14 day free trial but you need to input your card details to register. Once you have inserted your card details, hit subscribe.

8 If you wish to use Gemini Business, you will have the option to sign up for the Gemini Business add-on at this juncture. If you wish to use Gemini Enterprise, click skip for now.

9 If you wish to use Gemini Enterprise, go to admin.google.com

10 Sign into your workspace account (eg author@aicrimbook.com)

11 On the left hand side of the screen, click on 'Generative AI' and then 'Gemini'

12. Click on Service Status and click 'ON for everyone'

13 On the left hand side of the screen, click on the Home button.

14 Under 'Billing', click on 'Manage subscriptions'

15 Click on 'Add or upgrade a subscription'

16 Under 'categories' go to 'Gemini for Google Workspace'

17 Select Gemini Business or Gemini Enterprise (as you prefer).

As noted above, Gemini Business differs in that it has a cap on how many prompts you can ask Gemini per month. Once you have made your selection, click 'Get Started' and then 'Try for 14 days'. Gemini Enterprise is about £10 more expensive per month but allows you to submit unlimited prompts to Gemini.

18 Once you are all set, click on 'Start using Gemini' and then 'Chat with Gemini'.

19 Accept the terms and privacy conditions by selecting 'Use Gemini' and then 'Continue'.

Congratulations! You're all set up!

Google AI Studio

5.31 It is important to note that, if you use Google AI studio, you will be subject to additional payments depending on the model of Gemini you choose to use. The context or token limit you have is an important detail to consider when selecting your model; a token is approximately 4 characters meaning 100 tokens corresponds to 6-8 words[30].

5.32 When you want to ask Gemini to perform complex tasks, you will need to break the prompt down into steps so the model can build on the previous prompt (see next chapter for further details). The rate limit will dictate how many documents you can upload per prompt and how many consecutive prompts you can ask before you need to start a brand new request.

5.33 The standard model for AI Studio is Gemini 1.5 Flash[31]. This is offered free of charge but is subject to lower 'rate limits' (1 million context window) – this means that you can only ask a certain amount of questions per minute (15), and make a total of 1,500 requests per day. The tokens you can use with a given request are also limited; tokens represent the amount of CPU used to process your request. The Gemini 1.5 Flash has a limit of 1 million tokens per minute, which may make processing large documents difficult.

5.34 You can also opt to use the pay-as-you-go version of Gemini 1.5 Flash. This allows you to use 4 million tokens per minute or to make 2,000 requests per minute. within a single prompt per day before you have to start a new prompt. Prompts up-to 128k tokens cost $0.075 USD per 1 million tokens you input when requesting something of Gemini and $0.30 USD per 1 million tokens for any output generated for you up to 128k tokens. For Prompts longer than 128k tokens, you will be charged $0.15 USD per 1 million tokens you input in your prompts and $0.60 USD per 1 million tokens for the output generated in response.

5.35 Overall, we would recommend signing up for the pay-as-you go service for two reasons:

1 Your data associated with a paid service is not used to improve Google AI studio in any capacity;

2 You will be able to input more documents when asking prompts and/or get the model to generate more sophisticated outputs because you will have more tokens to avail of.

5.36 It is also important to note that, though Gemini 1.5 Flash is the standard, there are a number of Gemini models you can use. For further details, search for 'Google AI for Developers Pricing Models' or go to ai.google.dev/pricing

---

30 'About generative models,' *Google AI for Developers* <https://ai.google.dev/gemini-api/docs/models/generative-models?_gl=1*1aril1i*_up*MQ..*_ga*MTgyMjMwMDQwMy4xNzMwMTA1MjEx*_ga_P1DBVKWT6V*MTczMDEwNTIxMC4xLjAuMTczMDEwNTIxMC4wLjAuNzM1MDgyMjc.#prompting-versus>

31 'Pricing Models,' *Google AI for Developers* <https://ai.google.dev/pricing#1_5flash>

5.37 If you choose to use AI Studio, you will need to sign up for an API key. An API key is a unique identifier – an alphanumeric sequence – that allows a software developer to control who has access to their application programming interface (API)[32]. If you don't already have one (if you have never programmed before), you will need to create an API key in Google AI Studio.

5.38 To do this, follow the following steps:

1 Go to aistudio.google.com/app/apikey.

2 Make sure you are signed into your workspace account – it should appear on the bottom right corner of the screen under 'settings'. If you are signed into a different account, make sure to switch to your Google Workspace account (see steps above).

3 Click on 'Create API Key'.

4 Click on 'Create an API key in a new project'.

5 Google AI Studio will generate an API key for you – make sure you save your API key somewhere securely as anyone who has your API key can access your content on Google AI studio.

6 You will now be able to see your new API key listed in the window on the bottom of the screen. Alongside the API you will also see a project number, project name, and the date your API was created.

7 On the far bottom right, you will see a column called 'Plan'. There will be a link called 'Set up billing'. Click on this if you wish to use the paid version of Gemini for AI Studio.

8 If you choose to set up billing, you will be re-routed to Google Cloud. You may be asked to log into to your Workspace account.

9 You will then be asked to enable billing for project Gemini API – click on 'create billing account.

10 You will be asked to supply some account information – namely the country you are using Gemini in. Make sure your relevant country is selected (eg UK) and then click 'Agree and continue'.

11 You will then be asked for your payment information. You may input your VAT number and/ or relevant tax information at this stage. Insert the card information you wish to use to pay for your usage. Then click 'start free'.

---

32 According to IBM, an API key is, 'a unique identifier used to authenticate software and systems attempting to access other software or systems via an application programming interface, or API. An API, or application programming interface, is a set of rules or protocols that enable software applications to communicate with each other to exchange data, features and functionality. APIs give application owners a simple, secure way to make their application data and functions available to departments within their organization. Application owners can also share or market data and functions to business partners or third parties. APIs allow for the sharing of only the information necessary, keeping other internal system details hidden, which helps with system security.'
For further information, see the following explainers: https://www.ibm.com/think/topics/api-key ; or https://cloud.google.com/endpoints/docs

12 You will be asked to fill out some basic information about how you will use your Google Cloud account.

Your Google Cloud account will be used to save any prompts or outputs generated as you use Gemini for Google AI Studio.

13 Once you have finished setting up your account, you can exit the Google Cloud page and return to Google AI Studio.

You are now set up with AI Studio!

5.39 We would also recommend that you complete the following further step to access Gemini API for Enterprise on Vertex AI:

1 On the bottom right hand side you will be see 'Gemini API for Enterprise' – click on this link.

You do not have to use Gemini API for Enterprise but it is a good idea because you get over £250 free credits with your account and there are additional data protection elements associated with Enterprise accounts broadly (see above).

2 Click on 'Start your free Vertex AI trial'.

Congratulations! You are now fully set up!

5.40 To begin using Gemini on Vertex AI, go to 'Open Chat' under the banner that reads 'Generate with Gemini'.

CONCLUSION

5.41 Google Gemini offers some fantastic resources to help people become accustomed to using genAI. We would recommend checking out the following should you wish to explore genAI and/or Gemini on your own:

1 'About Generative models[33],' *Google AI for Developers*

2 *Gemini for Google Workspace: Prompting guide 101* (October 2024 edition)[34]

3 Google AI studio quickstart[35], *Google AI for Developers*

5.42 OpenAI, Anthropic, Meta, and Amazon AWS also offer incredible free resources that can help you select the LLM that best suits your needs. For the reasons set out above, it is essential to read the terms and conditions of Claude, ChatGPT, Gemini, and LLama before you make your selection.

33 <https://ai.google.dev/gemini-api/docs/models/generative-models?_gl=1*1aril1i*_up*MQ..*_ga*MTgyMjMwMDQwMy4xNzMwMTA1MjEx*_ga_P1DBVKWT6V*MTczMDEwNTIxMC4xLjAuMTczMDEwNTIxMC4wLjAuNzM1MDgyMjc.#prompt-types>

34 <https://workspace.google.com/learning/content/gemini-prompt-guide?utm_source=wgc&utm_medium=et&utm_content=wgc-geminipage-tile-handbook&utm_campaign=FY24-Q4-global-WKSP337-website-dl-gemini-advanced-ebook-gated-landing-page>

35 <https://ai.google.dev/gemini-api/docs/ai-studio-quickstart>

Chapter 6

Skeleton arguments, advices, submissions, conferencing, transcription, translation and talks

INTRODUCTION

6.01 Most criminal practitioners in England and Wales are time poor. In this chapter we look at practical ways in which AI may be used to speed up daily tasks, improve efficiency and improve the quality and accuracy of work. We break down the support we can derive from AI into two sections:

- writing skeleton arguments, advices, submissions, judgments and talks; and
- conferencing, transcription and translation.

6.02 This chapter aims to provide a comprehensive overview of how to use AI for written advocacy, advices, judgments and talks, offering practical guidance and step-by-step instructions for barristers, solicitors, and judges in England and Wales. The approach is necessarily subjective because AI may be used in myriad different ways. Examples are used to show what material might be uploaded to produce the most helpful result, what prompts might be used and what the product of the Large Language Model (LLM) looks like. This will enable the reader to decide to what extent a LLM might be useful and in respect of what tasks at this point in the development of AI.

6.03 The second part of the chapter is more straightforward, so conferencing, transcription and translation is addressed in shorter form.

SOURCE MATERIAL FOR CREATING QUASI-ORIGINAL WORK

6.04 With most legal drafting in criminal law, summarising the facts/factual background of the case takes the greatest proportion of the preparation time. In order to get AI to do this work for us we have to share evidence or documents from which the facts must be summarised with the AI model you are using for the task. As discussed in the previous chapter, when uploading material to a LLM, the data must not be available to be used for the processing of other people's tasks or there will be a risk of breaches of privilege, confidentiality and data protection obligations.

6.05 The paid version of Google Vertex is an example of an AI model that will not allow the data you upload to be scraped and/or shared; see **Chapter 5**. Practitioners and judges cannot simply use the free version of ChatGPT or Co-Pilot as the data inputted will be scraped.

6.06 The authors have found the LLMs within the paid versions of Google Vertex and AI Studio to be good functional AI models that protect your data; see the discussion on data in **Chapter 2**. It should also be noted that Google has developed NotebookLM[1]; powered by Gemini, this tool summarises files you upload (PDFs, audio, video etc) and makes 'connections between topics'. It also helps authors by providing citations for its work so that users can verify the exact quotes and sources it used in the formulation of its response. The Notebook tool, however, was released after the writing of this chapter and therefore was not used for the examples below.

6.07 LLMs available through AI Studio have been used for the examples in this chapter.

WRITING SKELETON ARGUMENTS, ADVICES, SUBMISSIONS, JUDGMENTS AND TALKS

What matters?

6.08 If using AI in the writing of skeleton arguments, advices, submissions, judgments and talks, four things matter: data protection (see above), accuracy, material and prompts.

6.09 It goes without saying that the product of AI work needs to be accurate. A combination of what material is uploaded and how prompts are drafted will inform the quality of the work output.

What to avoid?

6.10 If using a non-legal model, avoid simply asking for help without providing the model with material to draw from.

6.11 If you ask a LLM to plan a three-day holiday in Scotland in August incorporating Ben Nevis and Fingal's Cave, the advice you get may include driving to Edinburgh in time for a 'hearty meal' and driving to Skye to get a boat to Fingal's Cave. When the itinerary is checked by a human being, the reality is that no hotel is available in Edinburgh because it is August; and Fingal's Cave is in fact 186 miles from Skye – the model has mixed up Skye and Mull.

A MODULAR APPROACH

6.12 As human beings, we compartmentalise most aspects of case preparation, including the writing of case summaries, advices, judgments and speaking notes for oral advocacy. The

1 https://notebooklm.google/.

modules of an advice might be: 'introduction', 'summary of evidence', 'relevant law', 'analysis' and 'conclusion'. When using an AI model it is useful to break down the tasks for the writing of an advice into five modules, using these headings.

6.13 This has the advantage of the user being able to ask the model to perform one task at a time. That allows that task to be checked by the human being. It allows the prompt to be crafted carefully to perform one task to the best of the model's ability. The product is a self-contained module.

FACTUAL AND EVIDENTIAL SUMMARIES

6.14 Starting with a summary of evidence, one approach would be to compile a PDF bundle of witness statements and exhibits, upload that bundle into the AI model and then devise a prompt to prepare the summary of evidence.

Example in complex fraud

In a complex case, such as complex fraud, the case might naturally involve evidence which could be grouped into sections, including, eg: 'civilian and non-financial statements', 'financial statements concerning Trade 1' and 'financial statements concerning Trade 2'. The product is likely to be more coherent if the statements are uploaded in groups or sections.

For example, upload the civilian/non-financial statements as a compendious pdf into the model.

The prompt

There are different schools of thought on the optimal length of a prompt.

We suggest breaking the prompt down into short sentences. For legal writing, we have found that a prompt of about 60 words works well. Remember that the prompt is not the end of the interaction with the model.

For example:

In a small or moderately complex case:

> *Prepare a summary of the evidence contained in the attached witness statements. Make the summary detailed. Make it 100% accurate. Use the active, not the passive voice. Set all facts out in chronological order. Include in square brackets after each fact the surname of the witness from whose statement the fact derives, followed by a semicolon, followed by the pdf page number.*

Refining the prompt

It is worth bearing in mind that the output summary does not have to be achieved through a single prompt. Look at the output text and see if, and how, it needs refinement. A second prompt might be:

> *Now, make the paragraphs longer. Move text describing the events surrounding the arrest of X and the search which followed that to the beginning of the summary. Then set out in chronological order the events which were exposed by the investigation which followed the arrest and search. Summarise the defendant's police interview at the end of the case in a separate section headed 'Interview under caution'.*

A staged approach may yield better results, whereby an initial prompt is used to generate a first response and a further prompt may work well in refining that product.

Templates

Think about templates for each module you are preparing. Using the 'summary of evidence' example above, you could upload advices to be used by the model as templates.

Then enter the following modified prompt:

> *Prepare a summary of the evidence contained in the attached witness statements. Make the summary detailed. Make it 100% accurate. Use the active, not the passive voice. Set all facts out in chronological order. Include in square brackets after each fact the surname of the witness from whose statement the fact derives, followed by a semicolon, followed by the pdf page number. Emulate the style of language and sentence structure used in the summary of evidence sections in the three attached advices.*

Summarising media

The LLM may be used to summarise media. Examples follow.

Audio video evidence

Example where dialogue is important.

In a case involving tens of videos of segment of a vehicle's journey recorded on its own dashcam to show acts and declarations in support of a joint enterprise, it might be necessary for the prosecution to have a transcript of the dialogue between defendants. The prosecution could approach the preparation of the transcripts as follows:

Start by uploading one video at a time into the prompt box.

After each video is uploaded enter the following prompt:

From the attached video, set out the time at which something is said, followed by the words spoken. If the speech is from more than one person, set out the time, followed by a letter denoting the voice of the speaker, using a different letter for each speaker.

Model:

[00:00:00] A: I'm coming.

[00:00:01] B: Leave him.

[00:00:02] A: No, I'm not in my car.

[00:00:05] A: The car is hot inside, bro. Outside but I was sweating my whole car from my seat.

[00:00:11] B: Yeah, I'll be there in five minutes.

[00:00:13] A: [X] was meant to go right down, like, like, like, what's that road behind another one? Where you go [Y] College? And I was meant to go right there man and up that little roundabout, bro.

[00:00:22] B: Right there.

[00:00:24] A: Huh? Right there? Bro that road, what's that long road? When you come out now try the one-way bit when you come out what's that road called again?

[00:00:31] B: Don't know, bro.

[00:00:32] A: Bro, when you come out now try the exit, bro, at the back, bro.

[00:00:36] B: But

[00:00:37] A: I baffled, bro, I told him to go down there. This guy took me.

[00:00:40] B: Baffled.

[00:00:41] A: Baffled. [Y], [Y].

[00:00:43] B: [Y].

[00:00:44] A: Oh, shit.

[00:00:45] B: There's feds there, bro.

[00:00:47] A: Where? There, where then though?

[00:00:49] A: I'm in fucking, I'm by [Z], and coming. I just keep seeing baffled, baffled.

[00:00:52] B: I am saying that as well.

[00:00:58] A: Swear down, shit, I told you, bro.

In a matter of seconds, the prosecution has a full transcript of one video. The process can then be repeated. The transcript needs to be checked. The transcript, with the time marking, shows on what to hone in.

Example where human behaviour is important

Take the example of a CCTV video with no audio, where a description of what is captured is needed for a case summary concerning a charge of assaulting a police officer. Start by uploading the video. Then enter a prompt such as:

The attached video is CCTV footage which includes a brown-haired woman wearing high heels and a short black dress. When the video starts, she comes into shot from the right hand side of the screen. Summarise her behaviour throughout the video, by setting out the time displayed on the footage followed by what she did at that time.

Model

Sure, here is a summary of the brown-haired female's behaviour in the video:

[00:00:05] Appears into view and talks with two men and another female.

[00:00:08] Walks into the road and briefly hugs another female, who walks out of view.

[00:00:12] Starts a physical altercation with the female she hugged a moment ago, while the men intervene.

[00:00:33] Briefly disappears out of view before re-appearing.

[00:00:35] Walks along the pavement and talks to two other female people.

[00:00:40] Waves and moves her arms as she talks.

[00:00:45] Hugs another female.

[00:00:49] Speaks animatedly with a female, holding her hands.

[00:00:59] Walks across the road with another female, waving her arms.

[00:01:06] Approaches a man who is taking pictures of her and her companion.

[00:01:09] Walks across a pedestrian crossing.

[00:01:27] Hugs the man who is taking pictures, before being briefly grabbed by him.

[00:01:29] Continues walking with the other female.

[00:01:44] Starts another physical altercation with the female, before two men and other female people intervene.

[00:02:00] Kneels down on the ground before stumbling, and being helped back up by a man.

[00:02:08] Appears to push the other female, before the man intervenes again.

[00:02:33] Walks further down the road before police officers arrive at the scene.

[00:02:43] Walks off screen, before re-appearing at [00:02:46].

[00:02:50] Police officers surround her, holding both her arms.

[00:03:21] Gets into a police van.

[00:03:26] Runs back towards the original location of the altercation.

[00:03:33] A police officer takes her by the arm and leads her away.

Hopefully, this summary of the brown-haired female's behaviour was helpful.

Prompt 2

Describe in detail each physical altercation.

Model

There are three instances in the video that can be described as physical altercations involving the brown-haired woman:

1. ***[00:00:12-00:00:16]:*** The brown-haired woman and the other woman in the short dress appear to be arguing, and the brown-haired woman shoves the other woman. Two men quickly step in to separate them, holding the women back. The altercation is brief but clearly physical.
2. ***[00:01:44-00:02:00]:*** The brown-haired woman and the other woman engage in a more extended physical fight. It begins with shoving and escalates as they grapple with each other. A man intervenes and tries to break up the fight, pulling the brown-haired woman away. She falls to the ground, either from losing her balance or being pushed. The man helps her up, and the fight seems to pause momentarily.
3. ***[00:02:08-00:02:16]:*** The brown-haired woman lunges towards the other woman again, making physical contact. The same man from the previous altercation intervenes once more, pulling the women apart. It*'s unclear if the woman falls again or if she is pushed, but she ends up near the ground, and the man again assists her. This altercation is shorter than the second one, but still involves physical aggression. Shortly after, police officers arrive.*

It's important to note that the low resolution and quality of the CCTV footage make it difficult to determine the exact nature and intensity of each physical interaction with complete certainty. The descriptions above are based on the observable actions and body language of those involved.

What about self defence? A further prompt might help:

User

Are the police at any stage aggressive or violent?

Model

No, the police officers in the video do not exhibit any aggressive or violent behavior. Their actions appear to be aimed at de-escalating the situation and taking control. Here's a breakdown:

- ***[00:02:41-00:03:26]:*** The officers arrive and approach the brown-haired woman. They hold her arms, seeming to restrain her but not using excessive force. They engage in conversation, possibly trying to calm her down and understand the situation. She eventually enters a police vehicle.
- ***[00:03:33-00:03:37]:*** When the brown-haired woman runs back towards the scene, an officer intercepts her. He takes her by the arm and firmly guides her away from the area. The officer*'s actions seem preventative, aiming to prevent further conflict. There's no sign of violence or aggression.*
- ***[00:05:06-00:07:55]:*** In the final interaction captured in the video, officers are seen attending to what appears to be the same woman. The angle and quality of the footage obscure some details, but officers are seen kneeling beside the woman, perhaps providing assistance or further restraining her. Again, their actions appear calm and controlled, with no visible aggression.

Overall, the officers' demeanor and actions suggest a focus on managing the situation and ensuring the safety of those involved, without resorting to violence or aggression themselves. They appear to use reasonable force when necessary for restraint, but avoid any unnecessary escalation.

The practitioner may be interested in whether any words might have been said by the defendant on this video without audio. In this case the following check did not suggest that it might be possible to tell from the video. There may be other cases when a positive answer might inform the instruction of an expert.

User

Is it possible to tell what the brown-haired woman is saying at any stage by lip reading?

Model

Due to the low resolution and grainy nature of the CCTV footage, combined with the distance and angles of the camera, accurate lip reading is virtually impossible. The footage isn't clear enough to distinguish the subtle movements of the lips and tongue necessary for reliable interpretation. While we can observe the woman talking at various points, we can only speculate about the content of her conversations based on the surrounding context and body language.

Phone evidence

In a case where unlawful violence was alleged leading to the murder of female partner (B) by male partner (A), A alleged in mitigation that he (A) was the victim of coercive and controlling behaviour at the hands of B leading up to the killing. There were several thousand pages of telephone records of communications between them in separate phone reports. Can AI help? Start by uploading one report (before repeating with the others). Then, as an example, the following prompt could be used:

User

The attached phone report comprises or includes messages sent between a male romantic partner and female romantic partner. The male alleges that the female was coercive and controlling of him. Set out all messages which are or might be indicative of coercive or controlling behaviour. Contextualise them by including a sufficient number of messages either side to allow the reader to see the tone of the messages.

Model

The messages between the male ([Brian]) and female ([Eleanor]) reveal a complex dynamic that could be interpreted as containing elements of coercive and controlling behavior. It's important to note that this interpretation is based solely on the provided text messages and lacks the full context of their relationship.

1. ***One-sided Communication and Demands:*** Eleanor frequently makes demands or expresses displeasure without seemingly acknowledging Brian*'s input or feelings. This pattern emerges in several instances:*

- ***20/07/2021 14:31:*** *Eleanor: 'Why's WhatsApp not recording call timers?' Brian: 'No idea, this was over 3h' Eleanor: 'That's rubbish cuz we need that' Eleanor immediately dismisses Brian's response and asserts her need, without explanation.*
- ***20/07/2021 14:32:*** *Eleanor expresses dissatisfaction with Telegram and Viber, essentially dictating which communication platform Brian should use. Brian responds by suggesting she use Telegram in the future and explains he calls on PC sometimes. Eleanor does not directly acknowledge his responses, but continues directing him: 'That's rubbish cuz we need that / Telegram sucks, you're too quiet there / Unless you wanna dl viber.' Brian: 'I think it's ok on phone'. Eleanor doesn't reply.*

1. ***Potential Monitoring/Tracking Implication:*** The demand for call timers and Eleanor*'s concern about WhatsApp not recording them ('we need that') could be construed as a desire to monitor or track Brian's communication. This interpretation, however, requires additional context.*

2. ***Emotional*** *Manipulation:* Eleanor*'s statement, 'Telegram sucks, you're too quiet there,' suggests that Brian's behavior on a different platform is insufficient for her needs. This could be interpreted as an attempt to manipulate Brian into communicating more frequently or openly on a platform of her choosing.*

3. ***Unilateral Decisions about Communication Methods:*** Eleanor repeatedly dictates which messaging app Brian should use. She appears to dismiss his preferences or suggestions, creating an imbalance of power in the relationship dynamic.

It is important to consider the limitations of this analysis. The provided messages are snippets of a larger conversation history, and the full context is unavailable. Tone of voice, body language, and other non-verbal cues are missing, which are crucial for accurate interpretation. Additionally, the information is presented from the husband's perspective, and his interpretation of events may be influenced by his own feelings and experiences.

Ultimately, determining whether these behaviors constitute coercive control requires a more comprehensive understanding of the relationship dynamics and a detailed examination of the overall pattern of interactions between Brian and Eleanor. These messages alone provide some indicators, but they are insufficient to make a definitive conclusion.

6.15 The other reports in the example were more extensive and yielded more extensive hits.

6.16 This provided a platform for checking the nature and quality of the communication by reference to the examples.

SUMMARISING LAW

6.17 At the time of writing we do not recommend simply asking a non-law LLM to summarise law (from the internet).

Why not to ask the internet generally through the LLM

6.18 The Scottish holiday prompt (above) is writ large in this exchange, which is included in full, as it exposes the weaknesses in, and dangers of, simply 'asking the model'. No material was uploaded, so the model was to draw from the internet generally.

Prompt 1 (user entry)

Is there caselaw in England and Wales supporting the admissibility of disciplinary findings of professional tribunals in criminal courts?

Model

There is no clear-cut, singular caselaw in England and Wales definitively stating that disciplinary findings of professional tribunals are always admissible in criminal courts. However, there is a body of caselaw that provides guidance on when such findings may be admitted and the factors courts will consider.

Here's a breakdown:

General principles:

- ***Hearsay:*** Disciplinary findings are generally considered hearsay as they are statements made out of court offered to prove the truth of the matter asserted. Hearsay is inadmissible in criminal proceedings unless an exception applies.
- ***Exceptions:*** Several exceptions exist, including:
  - ***Res gestae:*** *Statements made close in time to the event in question.*
  - ***Admissions:*** *Statements made by the defendant that acknowledge their guilt.*
  - ***Statements against interest:*** *Statements made by someone against their own self-interest.*
  - ***Public documents:*** *Official documents created by public bodies.*
- ***Probative Value and Prejudicial Effect:*** Even if an exception applies, the court will still consider the probative value (relevance and weight) of the evidence and whether its prejudicial effect outweighs its probative value.

Case Law:

- ***R v. H (2002):*** This case concerned a teacher convicted of indecent assault. The court admitted the findings of the professional disciplinary panel, but emphasized that such findings are not conclusive proof of guilt and should be treated with caution.
- ***R v. R (2003):*** This case involved a doctor accused of sexual assault. The court allowed evidence of disciplinary findings from the General Medical Council to be admitted. However, it stressed the importance of caution and that the findings were not conclusive of the criminal charge.
- ***R v. B (2007):*** This case involved a doctor accused of sexual assault. The court admitted evidence of the disciplinary findings but emphasized the need for clear instructions to the jury on the weight to be given to such findings.

Key Considerations:

- ***Nature of the offence:*** The admissibility of disciplinary findings will depend on the nature of the criminal offence and the extent to which the disciplinary findings relate to it.
- ***Procedure of the disciplinary tribunal:*** Courts will consider the fairness of the procedure used by the disciplinary tribunal.
- ***Standard of proof:*** Disciplinary tribunals typically operate on a balance of probabilities standard, whereas criminal courts require proof beyond reasonable doubt.
- ***Weight given to findings:*** Judges will instruct juries that disciplinary findings are not conclusive proof of guilt and should be considered with caution.

Conclusion:

While no definitive caselaw exists, the weight of jurisprudence suggests that disciplinary findings of professional tribunals can be admissible in criminal proceedings. However, the admissibility will depend on the specific circumstances and the court will scrutinize the probative value and potential prejudice of such evidence. The court will also provide clear instructions to the jury on how to consider the evidence.

6.19 Above is a coherent, apparently sensible, answer which follows a broad summary of principles of evidence, which appear to be sufficiently accurate to make the user think that the cases might be helpful.

Prompt 2 (user entry)

What are the citations for those cases?

Model

You are right to ask for citations! It's important to have the specific references to check the case law yourself. Unfortunately, the cases I mentioned are not actual cases. I apologize for the error. [emphasis added].

It seems I have been mixing up real case law with examples and hypothetical scenarios. I am still under development and learning to provide accurate information.

To find actual case law on the admissibility of disciplinary findings in England and Wales, you can use legal databases like:

- ***Westlaw UK***
- ***LexisNexis UK***
- ***BAILII (British and Irish Legal Information Institute)***

You can search these databases using keywords such as:

- *'Disciplinary findings'*
- *'Professional tribunals'*
- *'Criminal proceedings'*
- *'Admissibility'*
- *'Hearsay'*

I hope this helps you find the relevant case law!

6.20 The danger of the user approach above is that the lawyer is lulled into a false sense of security by some broadly accurate statements of legal principle. One then sees the reference to the cases which are exactly what is required to advance a legal argument to the effect that the disciplinary findings are admissible in criminal proceedings. But for the second prompt, the user might have proceeded on the basis that the three cases existed and, whilst it would be necessary to find the citations later on, the case names could be read out in court.

Asking a non-law LLM for summaries of specific cases or texts

6.21 What works well is identifying a case or text from which principles may be drawn and asking the model to summarise them.

6.22 The following example uses *R v AFU* [2023] EWCA Crim 23; [2023] 1 Cr App R 16. This was a decision of the Court of Appeal Criminal Division (Carr LJ; McGowan and Goose JJ). The case considered the safety of convictions following an unequivocal guilty plea where the defendant was a victim of trafficking or modern slavery but their status as such had been overlooked by the police and parties in the Crown Court. It drew strands of principle together following the special court decision of *R v AAD* [2022] EWCA Crim 106; [2022] 1 Cr App R 19; [2022] 1 WLR. 4042 in which a series of questions posited by the Registrar of Criminal Appeals was answered.

6.23 Upload the report of the judgment to the model.

User

Attached is the case of AFU. Summarise the test to be applied by a prosecutor when considering whether or not to prosecute a possible victim of human trafficking or modern slavery who commits a criminal act. Set out the ratio decidendi of the case. Quote directly from the paragraphs setting out the core principles.

Model

Test to be applied by a prosecutor when considering whether or not to prosecute a possible victim of human trafficking or modern slavery (VOT):

The Court of Appeal in ***R v AFU*** highlighted the three-stage approach laid out in the relevant CPS guidance:

1. ***Identification:*** Prosecutors have a duty to make proper enquiries in criminal prosecutions involving individuals who may be VOTs by:
   - *Advising the investigating agency that it* ***must*** *investigate the suspect's trafficking situation; and*
   - *Advising that the suspect be referred to the National Referral Mechanism (NRM) regardless of early guilty plea indication.*
2. ***Defence of Duress:*** If there is clear evidence of a credible common law defence of duress (or a Section 45 defence under the Modern Slavery Act 2015), the case should be discontinued.

3. ***Public Interest:*** Prosecutors must consider if the offence was a direct consequence of, or committed in the course of, trafficking. If the suspect was compelled but not to the extent of duress, prosecution is generally ***not*** in the public interest, unless the offence was *'so serious' or aggravating features exist.*

Ratio Decidendi

The core principles outlined in ***R v AFU*** are as follows:

- ***Failure to comply with the CPS Guidance:***

  'It is clear that the police failed to discharge their duty as first responders and that the prosecution failed to comply with the Guidance.' (Para 135)

- ***Impact of compliance with Guidance:***

  'Had there been compliance with the Guidance, in the light of the fresh evidence, it can be seen that the following main pre-trial events would have been discovered by the prosecution authorities...' (Para 136)

- ***Abuse of Process:***

  'Thus, the unjustifiable failure on the part of the prosecution to take into account the Guidance led to material factors being overlooked.' (Para 137)

  'Armed with the fresh evidence it can be seen that the dominant force of compulsion was sufficient to reduce the applicant's criminality or culpability to or below a point where it was not in the public interest for him to be prosecuted and the applicant would or might well not have been prosecuted in the public interest.' (Para 138)

- ***Exceptional Cases and Unsafe Conviction:***

  'Taking all of the above into account and standing back, we conclude that, on the present combination of very unfortunate facts, this is one of those exceptional cases where there was a clear abuse of process such that the conviction is unsafe.' (Para 139)

  The court found that the failure of both the police and prosecution to identify and consider the defendant's circumstances as a potential VOT resulted in an abuse of process, rendering his conviction unsafe. The court emphasized the importance of following the CPS Guidance to ensure fair treatment of possible trafficking victims within the criminal justice system.

6.24 The above summary is satisfactory but refers to a three stage test. The test prosecutors have to apply is of critical importance in these cases. It is a *four stage* test in which the prosecutor must consider:

1 whether the defendant is a victim of modern slavery;

2 whether there is a credible defence of duress;

3 whether there is a credible modern slavery defence; and

4 the public interest (in a particular way by reference to compulsion with adult defendants).

6.25 The summary also fails to include a summary of how the public interest should be considered in such cases. In those circumstances, a second prompt might be in these terms.

Prompt 2 (User)

Clarify: isn't it a four stage test, not a three stage test? and what test is applied to see if prosecution is in the public interest?

Model:

You are absolutely correct. It is indeed a ***four-stage test****, not a three-stage test. My apologies for that oversight.*

Here's the full breakdown, clarifying the public interest element:

Four-Stage Test for Prosecuting Potential Victims of Trafficking (VOTs):

1. ***Initial Suspicion:*** Law enforcement officers must be alert to potential indicators of trafficking, both generally and specifically within the context of common VOT-related crimes like cannabis cultivation and immigration offences.
2. ***Investigation and Referral:*** If suspicion arises, a National Referral Mechanism (NRM) referral is mandatory. The investigating agency must investigate the individual*'s trafficking situation, regardless of early guilty plea indications or investigator opinions.*
3. ***Conclusive Grounds Decision:*** The Competent Authority makes a conclusive grounds decision on whether the individual is confirmed as a VOT.
4. ***Public Interest Test:*** Even if confirmed as a VOT, prosecution may still occur. The prosecutor applies a two-limb test considering:
   - ***Limb 1: Degree of Compulsion:*** *Was the criminal act a direct consequence of the trafficking, to the extent that culpability is significantly reduced?*
   - ***Limb 2: Broader Public Interest Factors:***
     - *Seriousness of the offence*
     - *Availability of alternatives for the defendant*
     - *Defendant's history and personal circumstances*
     - *Specifics of the crime and the defendant's role*
     - *Whether prosecution would deter future trafficking*

Prosecutorial Discretion: The ultimate decision to prosecute rests with the prosecutor, guided by CPS guidance and the factors above. The court will only intervene if the decision was 'clearly flawed,' such as failing to adequately consider the guidance or irrationally departing from a conclusive grounds decision.

The *R v AFU* case highlights the importance of the entire four-stage process, emphasizing that a failure at any stage, particularly regarding identification and referral, can lead to a miscarriage of justice. Even with a guilty plea, a conviction can be deemed unsafe if the proper process was not followed, especially when compelling evidence later emerges supporting the individual*'s claim of being a VOT.*

6.26 The above example provides a satisfactory summary of the legal principles deriving from the case. However, the model has made up a four stage test from other principles in the case. The well known four stage test will need to be added. On the other hand, it has summarised the principles relevant to public interest in a pithy way.

SUMMARISING LAW FROM PREVIOUS ADVICES (OR TEXT BOOKS)

6.27

User

The three attached advices are advices on the merits of leave to appeal against conviction and/ or sentence. Each contains a summary of the law under the heading 'Law' concerning the legal framework for applying for leave to appeal against conviction out of time for victims of human trafficking and modern slavery who commit criminal acts. Using the three advices as templates, summarise the law relevant to adults, not children, victims who commit criminal offences. Use the same writing style as that used in the advice templates.

Model

LAW

THE STATE'S DUTY TO IDENTIFY VICTIMS OF TRAFFICKING

The identification of victims of exploitation (slavery and trafficking) takes place in the United Kingdom via the National Referral Mechanism ('NRM'). First responders, such as police officers or social workers, who suspect that a person may be a victim of trafficking, refer the case to the Home Office for investigation. Officials first decide whether there are reasonable grounds to believe that the person may be a victim. If there are, he or she is usually given a period of 'recovery and reflection' during which money, practical assistance, and if necessary accommodation are provided. Not less than 45 days later (and nowadays usually much longer), the Home Office will make a 'conclusive grounds' decision as to whether the person is, on the balance of probabilities, a victim of trafficking. A conclusive grounds decision may be received by the Court of Appeal Criminal Division ('CACD') when it considers the safety of a conviction where a person's trafficking status has been overlooked or improperly considered in the Crown Court.

The decision as to whether or not a person is identified by the state as a VOT is made by reference to the definition of the offence trafficking in international law. Trafficking in international law does not require movement of people. It includes slavery and forced or compulsory labor. Trafficking is defined in the Palermo Protocol (article 3) and ECAT (article 4). The definition is refined in Directive 2011/36/EU.

S.45 MODERN SLAVERY ACT 2015

S.45(1) of the 2015 Act provides a statutory defense for VOTs who commit criminal acts: a person is not guilty of an offense if he is aged 18 or over at the date of the act which would otherwise be an offense, he does the act because he is compelled to do it, the compulsion is attributable to slavery or to relevant exploitation, and a reasonable person in the same situation as the person and having the person's relevant characteristics would have no realistic alternative to doing that act. The terms of the section 45 defense require that the person was 'compelled' to do the act, that the 'compulsion' is attributable to slavery or to relevant exploitation and that a reasonable person in the same situation would have had no realistic alternative. It is for the defendant to raise evidence of each of those elements and for the prosecution to disprove one or more of them to the criminal standard.

NON-PROSECUTION AND ABUSE OF PROCESS

By ECAT, article 26, the UK shall provide for the possibility of not imposing penalties on victims for their involvement in unlawful activities, to the extent that they have been compelled to do so. The CPS guidance interprets article 26 as a non-prosecution obligation underpinned by article 4, ECHR. The UK provides protection for VsOT under ECAT, article 26 in England and Wales through s.45. Where the prosecutorial decision was arguably impeachable on public law grounds, it could historically be challenged through an application for a stay of the proceedings based on abuse of process which gave a power of review of the prosecutorial decision. Following the coming into force of s.45, the abuse of process regime continues to apply.

There is no incompatibility in the availability of both a defense under s.45 and the abuse of process regime. Where CPS guidance has been complied with and any conclusive grounds decision has been appropriately considered, the court will not intervene merely because it disagrees with a decision to prosecute. Where CPS guidance has been disregarded, the court can intervene more readily. Similarly, where the prosecution has departed from a conclusive grounds decision without a rational basis for doing so, a prosecution may be stayed as an abuse of process. The court will review the decision to prosecute, considering rationality and procedural fairness.

INADEQUATE ADVICE AND SAFETY OF PLEAS

Guilty pleas will be vitiated if erroneous advice was given that was so strong as to go to the heart of the plea, such that it was not a true acknowledgment of guilt. An appeal can also succeed if the plea is vitiated by erroneous legal advice or a failure to advise as to a possible defense, even where the advice may not have been so fundamental as to have rendered the plea a nullity. In cases where the appellant has been adequately advised as to the availability of a s.45 defense and has nevertheless decided of his own free will to plead guilty, there will be no clear injustice, even where it is accepted that the s.45 defense would 'quite probably' have succeeded. Where some advice has been given but a defendant has not been enabled properly to understand the merits of his prospective defense, there may be a Boal clear injustice and/or the CACD will need to consider whether the plea was a nullity.

6.28 The above summary is a very good, succinct, statement of the relevant legal principles. In fact the summary of the essential elements of the defence and the operation of the evidential and legal burdens is a very economic, precise and accurate legal summary. It gives a very solid foundation for the summary of law to which additional elements could be added to render this component of a legal document fit for purpose.

ANALYSIS

6.29 Analysing the facts of a case against a legal framework is quintessentially the task of the lawyer applying their judgment to the case, whether it be practitioner or judge. The emphasis on particular matters is for the individual lawyer to assess and weigh. The product of that emphasis will inform the conclusion. So, in those circumstances, can a LLM help with analysis? Staying with the theme of the non-prosecution and defence of modern slavery victims shows how work in a previous case might be used for a current case.

User

The attached summary of evidence concerns a different, unrelated case to that for which the summary of law was necessary. This new case concerns a child not an adult.

Using the summary of the evidence, use the 'Analysis' sections of the three advices above as templates and prepare an analysis of whether or not the Applicant's conviction may be unsafe based on the law summarised in the three advices. The analysis should consider the following:

(1) whether there is sufficient evidence to say that the Applicant was harboured for exploitation in criminal activity;

(2) whether there is sufficient evidence of duress to say that if the prosecution had considered whether their case would have succeeded had the Applicant deployed the defence of duress there was or might well have been no realistic prospect of conviction;

(3) whether there is sufficient evidence of all of the limbs of the s.45 defence to say that if the prosecution had considered whether their case would have succeeded had the Applicant deployed the s.45 defence there was or might well have been no realistic prospect of conviction- analyse each limb of the defence separately;

(4) *whether this is a case which would or might well not have been maintained by the prosecution in the public interest if they had known all the circumstances of the Applicant's trafficking and exploitation.*

Model

ANALYSIS

1. *Harbouring for Exploitation in Criminal Activity:*

   The facts strongly suggest the Applicant was harbored for exploitation in criminal activity. He was found in a cannabis farm, a classic scenario for trafficking. He stated he was forced to look after the plants, owed a debt to traffickers, was provided with a phone (a common control tactic), given occasional money but not allowed to spend it, and was beaten when he tried to run away. The SCA's Conclusive Grounds decision explicitly states he was harbored and subjected to forced criminality.

2. *Duress:*

   While the facts show the Applicant was under pressure, duress requires immediacy of threat. The facts don't suggest the Applicant faced an immediate threat of death or serious injury at the time of the offense. While fear for his family's safety may have been a factor, it's unlikely a duress defense would have succeeded.

3. *s.45 Defense:*

   a) *Aged 18 or over: The Applicant turned 18 shortly before his arrest. The facts suggest the exploitation began before he turned 18. As such, the prosecution should have considered whether he met the criteria of s.45(4), the provision relevant to a person under 18, not s.45(1), the adult provision.*

   b) *Compelled to do the act: The Applicant states he was forced to look after the plants and feared being beaten if he didn't comply. The SCA's Conclusive Grounds decision supports this, finding he was a victim of forced criminality.*

   c) *Compulsion attributable to slavery or relevant exploitation: The Applicant's compulsion stemmed from his traffickingsituation, specifically debt bondage and forced criminality.*

   d) *No realistic alternative: The Applicant was a young Vietnamese national, isolated, controlled, and fearing for his and his family's safety. He had run away once and been caught and beaten, leaving him feeling trapped with no realistic alternative but to comply.*

4. *Public Interest:*

   This case involves a young person exploited by traffickers. While the offense is serious, the Applicant's vulnerability and the exploitative circumstances significantly reduce his culpability. Had the prosecution fully appreciated the Applicant's trafficking situation, particularly his age at the commencement of the exploitation, and applied s.45(4) not s.45(1) of the Modern Slavery Act, and the CPS Guidance (applying Joseph), they might well not have prosecuted in the public interest. The focus should have been on safeguarding and support for the Applicant, not prosecution. The public interest lies in protecting vulnerable individuals from exploitation, and prosecution in this case could be seen as undermining that interest. It is likely that the Court would respect the decision of the SCA. However, given that the Applicant was 17 at the material time of the exploitation the Court may require testing by appropriate questioning pursuant to s.45(4) of the Modern Slavery Act 2015, see R v AAD at [82], [84] and [108].

Given the Applicant's age, his history of trafficking and exploitation, the fact that this was his first criminal offence, the availability of support and rehabilitation outside of the criminal justice system and the nature of the offence, a prosecution would be unlikely in the public interest. If it were to be found that the prosecution was not an abuse of process the sentence would almost certainly be found to be unduly lenient. It would be open to the Court of Appeal Criminal Division to impose a Referral Order, as is the usual sentencing disposal for first time offenders under the age of 18. A custodial sentence was almost certainly unlawful, applying the principles of R v SC.

6.30 The model's answer is fascinating. The answer to the above question, '[C]an a LLM help with analysis?' is yes but the product of the LLM's 'work' should be treated with great care and used as no more than a template for the work of the lawyer. The text of the answer to question (1) is broadly accurate. It needs marshalling with different emphasis. With question (2) the model was given no assistance as to what duress is in law in England and Wales; yet its answer is good and could almost be adopted *verbatim*. The answer to question (3) is nuanced. The model has identified the change of age from 17 to 18 and the fact that the separate defences applied. The answers to question (3) imply that the Applicant would have had a s 45(4) defence (the defence which applies to children and/or s 45(1) defence (the adult defence). Aspects of the answer to question (4) might form the basis for discussion of this topic. There needs to be greater precision and elaboration of the analysis in the answer. The final paragraph is in two parts. The first sentence might be an appropriate conclusion by a lawyer looking at the facts of the case. The second part of the answer beginning 'If it were to be found that …' is meaningless and wrong incorporating a hallucination from the internet. Therefore, in terms of providing the structure for analysis, the LLM may help with aspects of the analysis. Ultimately it would have to be reworked by the user.

HARMFUL CONTENT

6.31 Where material raises red flags, such as harassment, hate, sexually explicit, dangerous content and/or civic integrity, a LLM may refuse to process an answer to a prompt. At the time of writing the user is given the option to – and may – adjust preset filters to enable the model to produce the answer. Lawyers may find that with cases involving subject matter like the child abuse of children or murder, the filters cannot be adjusted to produce a response at all.

LAW QUERIES OF LAW LLMS

6.32 AI-powered legal research platforms like LexisNexis® Practical Guidance, Westlaw Edge, and ROSS Intelligence can analyse legal databases and provide relevant case law, statutes, and legal analysis. These tools can help identify relevant authorities and streamline the research process. They should be excellent in eliminating citation hallucinations and should be more precise than non-legal LLMs. They will also be able to assist with billing, administration and aspects of practice management. In the fullness of time, it is likely that they will be able to help in the drafting of indictments and *pro forma* applications.

6.33 As an example, Lexis+ is a nascent model (a matter of months old at the time of publication), based on a large language generative AI concept. It will be developed to avoid functional and conceptual hallucinations. It uses Anthropic/Claude AI, open AI models and ChatGPT 4 to promote additional search capabilities, to break down prompts and uses retrieval-augmented generation (RAG), a technique for enhancing the accuracy and reliability of generative AI models with facts fetched from external sources. There is investment in commercial grade security for data protection. At the moment, the user can upload a 75 page document only for summarising or generating a draft email, letter, clauses, research notes or arguments. Following the prompt question, four more prompts may be inputted. The plan is for the user's documents to be held securely in a database personal to the user which can be used as a resource for AI based work.

6.34 To compare the functionality of Lexis+ with Google AI Studio, the same example question above was inputted into the model:

User

Is there caselaw in England and Wales supporting the admissibility of disciplinary findings of professional tribunals in criminal courts?

AI Assistant

Yes, there is caselaw in England and Wales supporting the admissibility of disciplinary findings of professional tribunals in criminal courts. According to Rule 32 of the Solicitors (Disciplinary Proceedings) Rules 2019, the judgment of any tribunal exercising a professional or disciplinary jurisdiction, whether in or outside England and Wales, may be proved by producing a certified copy of the judgment. The findings of fact upon which that judgment was based are admissible as proof, though not conclusive proof, of those facts SI 2019/1185 Solicitors (Disciplinary Proceedings) Rules 2019 (SI 2019/1185).

In the case of Hetherington and another v Solicitors Regulation Authority, it was noted that a professional disciplinary tribunal has specialist knowledge of the profession and its ethical standards. Therefore, its decisions on issues such as integrity must be respected unless there is an error in law Hetherington and another v Solicitors Regulation Authority.

Furthermore, in Regina (Fleurose) v Financial Services Authority, the Court of Appeal held that there is no distinction between civil and criminal proceedings when dealing with professional disciplinary proceedings. The admissibility of evidence obtained via questioning in such proceedings was upheld, indicating that the principles governing admissibility in civil proceedings apply similarly to disciplinary tribunals Regina (Fleurose) v Financial Services Authority – CSRC vol 25 iss 21/2.

Content supporting AI-generated response:

SI 2019/1185 Solicitors (Disciplinary Proceedings) Rules 2019 (SI 2019/1185) | UK Parliament SIs 2010-present | Statutory Instruments | Aug 6, 2019

Hetherington and another v Solicitors Regulation Authority | Judgments | Judgments | Oct 31, 2022

Regina (Fleurose) v Financial Services Authority – CSRC vol 25 iss 21/2 | CSR Case Reports | Case Reports | Dec 21, 2001

6.35 The above cases are not on point. With the *Fleurose* case, the judgment included discussion on whether disciplinary proceedings are civil or criminal in nature, which might give one the basis of an argument as to admissibility of disciplinary findings in criminal proceedings. It will be interesting to see how the functionality improves in the next months and years.

TALKS AND SLIDES

6.36 A LLM can be a great tool for writing talks and the accompanying text for slides.

6.37 For one part of a recent talk on expert witnesses it was necessary to marshal an example of how an expert might be tempted to be overly confident in their conclusions and how damaging that can be for their credibility in the case and in terms of potential reputational damage.

6.38 The case of *R v Choudhuri*[2] was a good example. In that case C had been represented at trial by a senior solicitor and KC, both highly respected. C was a medical doctor, ostensibly capable of running several medical clinics. When he was indicted with counts of fraud and perverting the course of justice over a significant time span, two psychiatrists were willing to opine on appeal that he had been unable to form the requisite *mens rea* for any of the offences because of his poor mental health; and he had been unfit to stand trial (although his doctor wife and lawyers had overlooked this). The Court of Appeal heard the evidence of the two psychiatrists and a separate

2 [2019] EWCA Crim 2341.

independent psychiatrist instructed by the Respondent Crown. The court preferred evidence of the prosecution expert. The court found the evidence of the first defence expert 'confused and unsatisfactory' and that the second did not support the propositions advanced by C.

User

Please draft PowerPoint slides and associated script for a 20 minute talk on expert witnesses. Use the judgment of Choudhuri as a case study to show that if forensic experts are unrealistically partisan, their judgement becomes impaired and their reputation can suffer. Summarise the facts of the Choudhuri case. *Then summarise the issues on appeal in the case. Then summarise separately the evidence of [Dr H], [Dr D] and [Dr C]. Then summarise the findings of the Court and why the Court found [Dr H] and [Dr D's] evidence to be confused and unsatisfactory. Then summarise why the court found [Dr C's] evidence to be realistic and impressive.*

Model

Expert Witnesses: A Case Study of Choudhuri

Slide 1: Title Slide

- ***Title:*** Expert Witnesses: Navigating Objectivity & Reputation
- ***Subtitle:*** A Case Study of Choudhuri
- ***Presenter:*** [Your Name]

(Script)

Good morning/afternoon everyone. Today, we'll delve into the crucial role of expert witnesses, exploring the vital importance of objectivity and the potential consequences of unrealistic partisanship. We'll use the case of R v Choudhuri as a compelling case study to illustrate these points.

Slide 2: The Choudhuri Case: Summary of Facts

- ***Heading:*** Setting the Scene: R v Choudhuri
- ***Bullet Point 1:*** In 2013, Dr. Abdul Choudhuri was convicted of fraud and perverting the course of justice.
- ***Bullet Point 2:*** The charges stemmed from an incident where Dr. Choudhuri found and kept a wallet containing a significant amount of cash.
- ***Bullet Point 3:*** Dr. Choudhuri subsequently engaged in elaborate attempts to cover up his actions, including fabricating evidence and influencing witnesses.

(Script)

The Choudhuri case involved a series of events that unfolded in 2010. Dr. Choudhuri, a qualified doctor, came across a lost wallet containing a substantial sum of money. Instead of returning the wallet, he decided to keep it and subsequently went to great lengths to conceal his actions.

These actions included fabricating alibis, attempting to influence witnesses, and even coaching a witness to lie under oath.

Slide 3: Issues on Appeal

- ***Heading:*** The Appeal: Challenging the Conviction
- ***Bullet Point 1:*** Dr. Choudhuri appealed his conviction, arguing that he was unfit to plead and stand trial due to undiagnosed paranoid schizophrenia.
- ***Bullet Point 2:*** He claimed his mental state at the time prevented him from forming the requisite intent for the crimes.
- ***Bullet Point 3:*** The appeal relied heavily on the evidence of three expert witnesses: Dr. H, Dr. D, and Dr. C.

(Script)

Dr. Choudhuri's appeal wasn't based on disputing the facts of the case but rather on challenging his mental capacity during the time of the offences and the trial. His legal team argued that his undiagnosed paranoid schizophrenia prevented him from understanding the charges against him and effectively participating in his own defense. This argument heavily relied on the testimony of three expert witnesses, each presenting their professional assessment of Dr. Choudhuri's mental state.

Slide 4: Expert Testimony: Diverging Opinions

- ***Heading:*** The Experts Weigh In: Dr. H & Dr. D
- ***Dr. H:***
  - ***Bullet Point 1:*** *Diagnosed Dr. Choudhuri with paranoid schizophrenia.*
  - ***Bullet Point 2:*** *Expressed 'significant concerns' about Dr. Choudhuri's fitness to plead.*
  - ***Bullet Point 3:*** *Suggested that Dr. Choudhuri's actions were driven by delusions and not dishonesty.*
- ***Dr. D:***
  - ***Bullet Point 1:*** *Agreed with the paranoid schizophrenia diagnosis.*
  - ***Bullet Point 2:*** *Expressed concerns about Dr. Choudhuri's capacity to form intent due to his mental state.*
  - ***Bullet Point 3:*** *Admitted a lack of clinical focus in assessing Dr. Choudhuri's motivations.*

(Script)

Both Dr. H and Dr. D, after examining Dr. Choudhuri, diagnosed him with paranoid schizophrenia. They presented evidence suggesting that his mental state could have impaired his judgment and capacity to form criminal intent. Their conclusions leaned towards attributing

Dr. Choudhuri's actions to his illness rather than calculated dishonesty. However, both experts admitted certain limitations in their assessments, particularly in directly correlating his mental state to the specific mental elements of the crimes.

Slide 5: Expert Testimony: A Different Perspective

- ***Heading:*** The Counterpoint: Dr. C
- ***Bullet Point 1:*** Dr. C, instructed by the prosecution, also reviewed the case materials.
- ***Bullet Point 2:*** He acknowledged the possibility of retrospective diagnosis but highlighted its limitations.
- ***Bullet Point 3:*** He found Dr. Choudhuri*'s ability to engage in complex legal proceedings and give detailed evidence at trial to be inconsistent with claims of incapacity.*

(Script)

Dr. C, brought in by the prosecution, offered a different perspective. While acknowledging the diagnosis of paranoid schizophrenia, he emphasized the inherent complexities and limitations of retrospective assessments of fitness to plead. He pointed to Dr. Choudhuri's conduct during the investigation and trial, particularly his ability to comprehend complex legal arguments and actively participate in his own defense. This, he argued, contradicted the claims of incapacity put forth by the defense.

Slide 6: The Court's Findings

- ***Heading:*** The Judgment: A Question of Objectivity
- ***Bullet Point 1:*** The Court found Dr. H and Dr. D*'s evidence to be 'confused and unsatisfactory.'*
- ***Bullet Point 2:*** The Court criticized their reliance on Dr. Choudhuri and his wife*'s potentially unreliable accounts.*
- ***Bullet Point 3:*** The Court praised Dr. C*'s evidence for its objectivity and focus on the legal criteria for fitness to plead.*
- ***Bullet Point 4:*** Ultimately, the Court upheld the conviction, finding no arguable basis to conclude Dr. Choudhuri was unfit to plead.

(Script)

The Court ultimately found the evidence presented by Dr. H and Dr. D unconvincing. The judgment criticized their overreliance on the accounts provided by Dr. Choudhuri and his wife, which the court deemed potentially unreliable. Additionally, the court highlighted the lack of a clear nexus between the diagnosed mental illness and the specific mental elements required for the crimes committed.

In contrast, the Court commended Dr. C's evidence for its focus on the legal criteria for fitness to plead and his objective assessment of Dr. Choudhuri's capabilities during the trial. Therefore, the Court upheld the original conviction, rejecting the appeal based on unfitness to plead.

Slide 7: Lessons Learned: The Importance of Objectivity

- ***Heading:*** The Takeaway: Upholding Impartiality & Expertise
- ***Bullet Point 1:*** Choudhuri exemplifies the critical need for expert witnesses to maintain objectivity.
- ***Bullet Point 2:*** Unrealistic partisanship can lead to flawed conclusions, harming both the case and the expert*'s reputation.*
- ***Bullet Point 3:*** A focus on the evidence, the relevant legal criteria, and an objective approach are essential for maintaining credibility and ensuring justice.

(Script)

This case serves as a stark reminder of the paramount importance of objectivity for expert witnesses. When experts allow personal biases or a desire to advocate for one side to overshadow their professional judgment, their conclusions become susceptible to error. This can have far-reaching consequences, impacting not only the outcome of the case but also the expert's hard-earned reputation. The Choudhuri case underscores the crucial role of expert witnesses in the legal system and the need to uphold the highest standards of objectivity and professionalism.

Slide 8: Questions?

- ***Heading:*** Thank You. Questions?

(Script)

Thank you for your time. I am happy to take any questions you might have.

6.39 The talk needed a deal of nuanced shaping after that result but it may immediately be seen that with the right resource uploaded and some careful consideration for the terms of the prompt, the result will save a significant amount of time on the preparation of a talk.

PREDICTIVE ANALYTICS AND CASE OUTCOME PREDICTION

6.40 AI tools can analyse historical case data and identify patterns that can predict potential outcomes. These insights can be valuable in developing legal strategies and preparing arguments. As to how to use a LLM in order to model outcome prediction, the analysis section above shows how legal analysis might be informed by the use of a LLM. Uploading cases of a particular court or constitution and devising a prompt relevant to likely outcome might inform advice as to the merits of a case by reference to likely outcome.

TRANSCRIPTION, TRANSLATION AND CONFERENCING

6.41

- AI-powered platforms like Zoom, Microsoft Teams, and Google Meet offer features like real-time transcription, translation, and noise cancellation, enhancing collaboration and communication.

- **Transcription Software:** AI-powered transcription services like Otter.ai, Trint, and Descript can accurately transcribe audio and video recordings, saving time and effort. Alternatively, by recording a meeting, uploading the audio (or AV) file to a LLM and asking for a transcript, an after the event transcript may be prepared within seconds.
- **Translation Services:** AI-powered translation services like Google Translate, DeepL, and Microsoft Translator can facilitate communication across language barriers, allowing for international legal collaboration. The processing speed and accuracy of Google Translate, for example, at least with certain languages, are so good that although a translator needs to check the work, the idiom is sometimes better than that of a human translator. It is an invaluable tool for those prosecuting and defending in cases involving vast quantities of telephone communication media.
- **Conferencing:** AI may be used to Schule meetings automatically, it can transcribe in real time, or after recording meetings. AI can be used to transcribe the recording and structure it into a chapter-organised document. AI may be used to highlight key information and generate actions for participants.
- AI can transform your meetings by automating many tasks. It can schedule meetings at convenient times, transcribe discussions in real time, and create summaries afterward. AI is used to improve audio and video quality. It may be used to filter out distractions. Participant engagement may be augmented by highlighting speakers and generating live captions.

CONCLUSION (BY AI)

6.42

> *AI is revolutionizing the legal profession, offering powerful tools to enhance efficiency and improve the quality of legal services. This chapter has explored the use of AI in writing skeleton arguments, advices, and submissions, as well as in conferencing, transcription, and translation.*
>
> *By embracing these technologies, legal professionals can streamline workflows, improve communication, and enhance their ability to provide effective legal representation. However, it is crucial to approach AI with a critical eye, recognizing its limitations and ethical implications. By carefully considering the benefits and challenges, legal professionals can harness the power of AI to elevate the practice of law in England and Wales.*

6.43 To the model's conclusion, it is worth adding that the product of LLMs includes hallucinations and errors, as have been seen in the exemplars used as case studies above. It goes without saying that practitioners and judges using AI need to check every detail themselves for accuracy.

Chapter 7

AI and/in the judiciary

7.01 The legal system is one of the largest ‘text processing industries’ given its reliance on documents and data[1]. The digitisation of court documents, statutes and regulations, legal textbooks, government guidance and white papers, and law reports – particularly since Covid-19 – has made it increasingly easy to integrate AI into judicial proceedings. The appeal of doing so is obvious: with its ability to process thousands of documents and data points in minutes, the technology promises to reduce workload and improve the running of a system that is overburdened, underfunded, and overworked[2]. It is unsurprising, then, that in December 2023, the Courts and Tribunals Judiciary published the first Judicial Guidance on AI[3]. The introduction frames the importance of the practical guidance by remarking that, as AI’s importance to society continues to grow, so does its relevance to the court and the tribunal system[4].

7.02 In this chapter, we will explore the ways in which AI is already being used by judicial systems internationally before turning to risks that courts and tribunals should be aware of when using AI and/or dealing with AI generated content in the UK.

OVERVIEW

7.03 The use of AI in UK courts is still in its early stages and is largely limited to research and administrative tasks. The ways in which is already being deployed include, but are not limited to:

1 Technology assisted review (TAR)

2 Case management in the courts

3 Transcription and translation

4 Predictive analytics

1 Eckard Schindler, ‘Judicial systems are turning to AI to help manage vast quantities of data and expedite case resolution,’ *IBM.com Blog* (8 January 2024) <https://www.ibm.com/blog/judicial-systems-are-turning-to-ai-to-help-manage-its-vast-quantities-of-data-and-expedite-case-resolution/>

2 Keri Grieman, ‘Judge Dread: AI and Judicial Integrity,’ *United Nations Office on Drugs and Crime* (2021) <https://www.unodc.org/dohadeclaration/en/news/2021/30/judge-dread_ai-and-judicial-integrity.html>

3 ‘ Artificial Intelligence (AI) – Judicial Guidance,’ *Courts and Tribunals Judiciary* (12 December 2023) <https://www.judiciary.uk/guidance-and-resources/artificial-intelligence-ai-judicial-guidance/>

4 ‘Artificial Intelligence (AI) – Judicial Guidance,’ *Courts and Tribunals Judiciary* (12 December 2023) <https://www.judiciary.uk/guidance-and-resources/artificial-intelligence-ai-judicial-guidance/>

5 Judgment writing

6 Sentencing and probation

TECHNOLOGY-ASSISTED REVIEW

7.04 AI systems are already being used to identify potentially relevant documents as part of electronic disclosure in the UK[5]. TAR, also known as 'computer-assisted review' or 'predictive coding', is an electronic tool whereby legal teams can use AI to predict the likelihood of a document's relevance to a particular case or matter[6]. As the legal team reviews a sample of the documents being considered for disclosure and manually mark which ones are relevant, the system learns the criteria for selection and is then able to predict relevance across the remaining data set.

7.05 The use of TAR, Technology Assisted Review, for disclosure in Civil/ Commercial Proceedings was approved by the High Court in 2016; in *Pyrrho Investments Ltd v MWB Property Ltd,* the court extolled the virtues of using TAR, based partly on case-studies from the USA and Ireland where courts had been using the technology successfully since 2012[7]. This decision was affirmed and expanded upon in *Brown v BCA Trading*[8]. Despite the fact that an application was brought against using predictive coding in judicial proceedings (the claimant argued 'unfair prejudice'), the High Court endorsed TAR for large disclosure exercises where predictive coding would be the 'most reasonable and proportionate method of disclosure[9].'

7.06 In terms of Criminal Proceedings, the Crown Prosecution Service's (CPS) Legal Guidance for Disclosure 2022 confirms that, where there is a large volume of material that disclosure officers and/or investigators need to sift through for disclosure, 'it is perfectly proper for the investigator and/or disclosure officer to search by sample, key words, or other appropriate search tools or analytical techniques to locate relevant passages, phrases and identifiers[10].' More recently, in 2024, the *Attorney General's Guidance on Disclosure* also endorsed the use of TAR for examining and reviewing material for disclosure purposes in criminal proceedings[11].

---

5 'Artificial Intelligence (AI) – Judicial Guidance,' *Courts and Tribunals Judiciary* (12 December 2023) <https://www.judiciary.uk/guidance-and-resources/artificial-intelligence-ai-judicial-guidance/>, p. 2

6 'Disclosure: Technology Assisted Review and the Courts – Where are we now?', *Clifford Chance* (2018) <https://www.cliffordchance.com/content/dam/cliffordchance/briefings/2018/03/disclosure-technology-assisted-review-and-the-courts-where-are-we-now.pdf>

7 *Pyrrho Investments Ltd v MWB Property Ltd* [2016] EWHC 256 (Ch), *Westlaw UK* <https://uk.practicallaw.thomsonreuters.com/D-036-4782?transitionType=Default&contextData=(sc.Default)>

8 [2016] EWHC 1464 (Ch), *Westlaw UK* <https://uk.practicallaw.thomsonreuters.com/D-100-0861?transitionType=Default&contextData=(sc.Default)>

9 Alan Watts, 'Predictive coding ordered despite party's objections,' *Herbert Smith Freehills* (11 July 2016) <https://www.herbertsmithfreehills.com/notes/litigation/2016-07/predictive-coding-ordered-despite-partys-objections>

10 Disclosure Manual: Chapter 30 – Digital Material, *CPS Legal Guidance* (14 July 2022) <https://www.cps.gov.uk/legal-guidance/disclosure-manual-chapter-30-digital-material>

11 Para 41, *Attorney General's Guidelines on Disclosure: For investigators, prosecutors and defence practitioners* (2024) <https://assets.publishing.service.gov.uk/media/65e1ab9d2f2b3b00117cd803/Attorney_General_s_Guidelines_on_Disclosure_-_2024.pdf>

CASE MANAGEMENT

7.07 The Council of Europe's CEPEJ (European Commission for the evaluation of justice) has created a publicly accessible database that documents the AI systems and other cybertools being deployed by judiciaries around the world[12]. As of October 2024, there were 118 AI systems being deployed in judiciary systems internationally.

7.08 A prime example of such a system is being deployed in Brazil. There, the Supreme Court has adopted a case management system called VICTOR that processes the thousands of appeals brought to court to identify cases that meet the 'general repercussion' prerequisite or what Brazilian legislation calls 'Topics of General Repercussion'[13].

7.09 The Internet Court in Hangzhou, China, however, has taken the use of AI even further. They have adopted an evidence analysis system that uses blockchain technology, AI, big-data, and cloud computing to analyse and compare all the evidence presented by the parties in a dispute[14]. The system then compiles its analysis into a list of evidence and relevant exhibits, sorting the evidence into user-friendly visuals and summaries for a human judge to review.

TRANSCRIPTION AND TRANSLATION

Transcription

7.10 The AI legal transcription industry is already booming with projections showing it will be worth over $3 billion USD worldwide by 2029[15]. As of the time of writing, AI systems can already automatically transcribe spoken words into written text, creating increasingly accurate and searchable records of court proceedings, depositions, and other legal events.[16] There are a number of benefits to deploying this technology, including:

1 It significantly reduces the time and cost associated with manual transcription.

12 'Resource Centre on Cyberjustice and Artificial Intelligence,' *Resource Centre Cyberjustice and AI by CEPEJ* <https://public.tableau.com/app/profile/cepej/viz/ResourceCentreCyberjusticeandAI/AITOOLSINITIATIVESREPORT?publish=yes>

13 Eduoardo Villa Coimbra Campos, 'Artificial Intelligence, the Brazilian Judiciary and Some Conundrums,' *SciencesPo.fr* (3 March 2023) <https://www.sciencespo.fr/public/chaire-numerique/en/2023/03/03/article-artificial-intelligence-the-brazilian-judiciary-and-some-conundrums/>

14 F Bell and others, 'AI Decision-Making and the Courts: A Guide for Judges, Tribunal Members and Court Administrators' (Australasian Institute of Judicial Administration 2022); UNESCO, 'Global Toolkit on AI and the Rule of Law for the Judiciary' (The United Nations Educational, Scientific and Cultural Organization (UNESCO) 2023) CI/DIT/2023/AIRoL/01 <https://unesdoc.unesco.org/ark:/48223/pf0000387331> , p. 55

15 Beth Worthy, 'Decoding the Future of Legal Transcription: AI Versus Human,' (21 July 2023) *Forbes.com* <https://www.forbes.com/councils/forbesbusinesscouncil/2023/07/21/decoding-the-future-of-legal-transcription-ai-versus-human/>

16 Duran Ross and Nicola Thompson, 'The role of AI in the civil courts of England and Wales: a new era of justice,' (7 November 2024) *Lewis Silkin Dispute Resolution blog posts* <https://disputeresolution.lewissilkin.com/post/102jno4/the-role-of-ai-in-the-civil-courts-of-england-and-wales-a-new-era-of-justice>

2 Real-time transcripts can be used to generate closed captions for live-streamed court proceedings to aid individuals with hearing impairments[17]. AI tools have become sophisticated enough to handle multiple speakers, accents, and dialects meaning accuracy of these transcripts is increasing.

3 Digital transcripts can be searched for relevant keywords, phrases, and specific testimonies thus facilitating legal research and speeding up case preparation. A prime example of an AI tool currently being used to transcribe legal cased into searchable and structured text is Transkit, developed by the Basque Government Informative Society (EJIE) and deployed in 2023[18].

7.11 Though the benefits are notable, the technology is far from perfect and stakeholders have raised a number of concerns regarding its deployment in court. Among the most common objections are:

1 **Accuracy with complex legal terminology:** Legal language can be complex and nuanced, containing specific terminology and important context-dependent statements that can be challenging for AI systems to accurately transcribe[19]. While human transcribers can stop proceedings to ask clarifying questions, AI systems cannot, meaning they may generate seemingly plausible but inaccurate transcripts of proceedings[20].

2 **Disambiguation of speakers in noisy environments:** Though the technology has much improved, accurately identifying and attributing speech to the correct speaker can still be challenging, especially when there are overlapping conversations or interruptions. Courtrooms and deposition rooms can be noisy, with background chatter, echoes, and other audio distractions that can interfere with the accuracy of transcription. AI systems may also struggle properly to interpret cultural references, idiomatic expressions, or dialects[21].

3 **Maintaining data security and confidentiality:** By late 2023, at least 21 US Federal trial judges had issued standing orders against using AI in court proceedings until more data can be gathered about the implications of using AI in court and the accuracy of the technology further improves[22].

17 'Ai in the Courtroom: revolutionizing translation and transcription methods' (6 August 2024) *Almawave.com* <https://www.almawave.com/ai-in-the-courtroom-revolutionizing-translation-and-transcription-methods/#:~:text=Transcription%20in%20the%20Courtroom,-In%20the%20modern&text=These%20tools%20leverage%20advanced%20speech,methods%20reliant%20on%20human%20stenographers.>

18 'Speeding up judicial proceedings with Transkit, and AI-based tool that transcribes trials,' *Interoperable Europe (European Commission)*

19 Michael Murray, 'The Rise of AI in Court,' (12 January 2024) *Law.com* <https://www.law.com/legaltechnews/2024/01/12/the-rise-of-ai-in-court-reporting-technology/>

20 Ben Walker, 'AI is not the Answer: The Case for Human Court Transcriptionists,' (18 October 2024) *Law.com* <https://www.law.com/therecorder/2024/10/18/ai-is-not-the-answer-the-case-for-human-court-transcriptionists/?slreturn=20241216122031>

21 Michael Murray, 'The Rise of AI in Court,' (12 January 2024) *Law.com* <https://www.law.com/legaltechnews/2024/01/12/the-rise-of-ai-in-court-reporting-technology/>

22 David Lat, 'AI Use in Law Practice Needs Common Sense, Not More Court Rules,' (28 February 2024) *Bloomberg Law* <https://news.bloomberglaw.com/us-law-week/ai-use-in-law-practice-needs-common-sense-not-more-court-rules>

Translation

7.12

1 **Real-time translation in court:** AI-powered translation tools can provide real-time translation of spoken language in court, allowing non-native speakers to understand the proceedings and participate effectively. Indeed, translation services make legal information accessible to a wider range of individuals, including those who speak different languages or have visual impairments.

2 **Translation of legal documents:** AI can translate legal documents, contracts, and other written materials quickly and efficiently, facilitating translation of historical legal documents[23], cross-border legal transactions, and international collaborations.

Challenges of AI translation in legal settings

7.13

1 **Nuances of legal language and cultural differences:** As previously mentioned, legal terminology and phrasing is highly specialised and context-dependent. Accurately translating legal terms and concepts requires paraphrasing a word or statement from the original language accurately to convey its meaning – eg because the legal terminology is absent in the other language. Literal translations are often misleading or inaccurate precisely because effective translation requires working 'between two languages and two cultures while also navigating two co-existing legal systems with different legal concepts and terminology'.[24]

2 **Maintaining accuracy and precision:** Translating legal documents requires meticulous attention to meaning; errors in translation can have significant legal consequences. Human review and verification are still essential to ensure accuracy, particularly given the possibility of hallucinations[25].

3 **Confidentiality and data security:** As with transcription, many are concerned about entrusting confidential documents and privileged information to AI systems. A system breach, a hack, or a simple data security failure could have severe consequences for the integrity of the judicial process[26].

---

23 Luis Millán, 'AI is not the panacea to translate court rulings,' (30 August 2024) *Canadian Bar Association – The National Magazine* <https://nationalmagazine.ca/en-ca/articles/law/hot-topics-in-law/2024/ai-is-not-the-panacea-to-translate-court-rulings>

24 Luis Millán, 'AI is not the panacea to translate court rulings,' (30 August 2024) *Canadian Bar Association – The National Magazine* <https://nationalmagazine.ca/en-ca/articles/law/hot-topics-in-law/2024/ai-is-not-the-panacea-to-translate-court-rulings>

25 Luis Millán, 'AI is not the panacea to translate court rulings,' (30 August 2024) *Canadian Bar Association – The National Magazine* <https://nationalmagazine.ca/en-ca/articles/law/hot-topics-in-law/2024/ai-is-not-the-panacea-to-translate-court-rulings>

26 Zach Warren, 'Court personnel remain unsure about Gen AI usage, want accuracy assurances,' (29 February 2024) *Thomson Reuters* <https://www.thomsonreuters.com/en-us/posts/technology/gen-ai-court-usage/>

PREDICTIVE ANALYTICS

7.14 Some AI systems are capable of analysing data from hundreds of past cases to predict the likely outcomes of litigation or sentencing[27]. These AI systems use data mining, machine learning, and statistical modeling to analyse historical legal data – decisions, statutes, regulations, trends in jury behaviour etc – to determine how a particular court, jury, or tribunal is likely to interpret the facts and/or apply the law.

1 **Litigation outcome prediction**: By analysing data points from similar past cases, such as the judge assigned, the legal issues involved, the strength of evidence, and the jurisdiction, AI algorithms can attempt to predict the likelihood of success for a particular party, the potential damages awarded, or the duration of the litigation process. This can inform litigation strategy, settlement negotiations, and resource allocation – for example by pinpointing which arguments have historically succeeded in certain courts, indicating the strengths/weaknesses of opposing counsel and their preferred strategy in similar matters, or by helping legal practitioners better advise their clients so that they can make ever-more informed decisions[28].

2 **Sentencing prediction**[29]: This controversial application aims to predict the likelihood of recidivism or the appropriate sentence based on factors like the offender's criminal history, demographics, and the nature of the crime. Proponents of the technology argue that it will allow for more neutral and objective sentencing, particularly when decisions consider the likelihood of criminal recidivism.

7.15 However, predictive analytics are a highly sensitive and hugely contested area of innovation. There are serious ethical concerns about potential bias embedded in the data used to train these systems:

1 **Bias in training data**: The biggest challenge is the potential for bias in the algorithms. If the historical data used to train the AI system reflects existing biases in the legal system (eg, racial or socioeconomic disparities in sentencing), the system will likely perpetuate and even amplify those biases, under the guise of 'machine-neutrality'[30].

2 **Transparency and explainability**: The 'black box' nature of some AI algorithms makes it difficult to understand how they arrive at their predictions. This lack of transparency raises

27 Ashley Hallene and Jeffrey M Allen, 'Using AI for Predictive Analytics in Litigation,' (16 October 2024) *American Bar Association* <https://www.americanbar.org/groups/senior_lawyers/resources/voice-of-experience/2024-october/using-ai-for-predictive-analytics-in-litigation/>

28 Ashley Hallene and Jeffrey M Allen, 'Using AI for Predictive Analytics in Litigation,' (16 October 2024) *American Bar Association* <https://www.americanbar.org/groups/senior_lawyers/resources/voice-of-experience/2024-october/using-ai-for-predictive-analytics-in-litigation/>

29 Harry Grindle, 'The Techno-Judiciary: Sentencing in the Age of Artificial Intelligence,' *Sentencing Academy* <https://www.sentencingacademy.org.uk/sentencing-in-the-age-of-artificial-intelligence/>

30 Harry Grindle, 'The Techno-Judiciary: Sentencing in the Age of Artificial Intelligence,' *Sentencing Academy* <https://www.sentencingacademy.org.uk/sentencing-in-the-age-of-artificial-intelligence/>

concerns about due process and defendants' ability to appeal (or otherwise challenge) the basis of a prediction[31].

JUDGMENT WRITING

7.16 Building upon predictive analytics, GenAI has already been used to author a number of judgments. In Europe, the Frankfurt District Court in Germany has been testing an AI system called the Frankfurt Judgment Electronic Configurator ('Frauke') to draft civil judgments in airline passenger rights proceedings [32]. The court sees between 10,000-15,000 passenger rights cases a year and the judgments are often almost identical in their legal bases, wording, etc. In a proof of concept conducted in 2023, the system successfully extracted individual case-data (eg flight numbers and delay times) from the pleadings and, using pre-written text modules and the judge's verdict, it was able to draft judgments for human review[33].

7.17 In Colombia, the judiciary has begun implementing the technology to author judicial opinions. In January 2023, Judge Juan Manuel Padilla used ChatGPT to research and partly author a judgment addressing a petitioner's request for a waiver of their health insurance fees for her autistic child's medical treatment[34]. Less than two weeks later, Judge Maria Victoria Quiñones of the Administrative Tribunal in Colombia used legal and technical research conducted via ChatGPT to validate the decision to hold a hearing in the Metaverse[35] – a fully virtual reality not to be confused with videoconferencing – as well as to create procedural rules on how a virtual court appearance would be conducted[36]. Both of these cases are examples of instances in which GenAI has been used to answer technical and/or legal questions fundamental to disputes before the court; AI was being applied to parse and interpret the law and not just regurgitate facts.

7.18 Admittedly, the UK judiciary has taken a more conservative approach to integrating and/or consulting GenAI when preparing judicial opinions. The recent Judicial Guidelines for AI do not, however, preclude their using AI systems: 'Judicial office holders are personally responsible for material which is produced in their name. Judges are not generally obliged to describe the research or preparatory work which may have been done in order to produce a judgment. Provided

31 Harry Grindle, 'The Techno-Judiciary: Sentencing in the Age of Artificial Intelligence,' *Sentencing Academy* <https://www.sentencingacademy.org.uk/sentencing-in-the-age-of-artificial-intelligence/>

32 Eckard Schindler, 'Judicial systems are turning to AI to help manage vast quantities of data and expedite case resolution,' *IBM.com Blog* (8 January 2024) <https://www.ibm.com/blog/judicial-systems-are-turning-to-ai-to-help-manage-its-vast-quantities-of-data-and-expedite-case-resolution/>

33 Eckard Schindler, 'Judicial systems are turning to AI to help manage vast quantities of data and expedite case resolution,' *IBM.com Blog* (8 January 2024) <https://www.ibm.com/blog/judicial-systems-are-turning-to-ai-to-help-manage-its-vast-quantities-of-data-and-expedite-case-resolution/>

34 Brittan Heller and Daniel Castaño, 'Artificial Intelligence, Virtual Courts, and Real Harms,' *Lawfare* (13 March 2023) <https://www.lawfaremedia.org/article/artificial-intelligence-virtual-courts-and-real-harms>

35 Juan David Gutiérrez, 'ChatGPT in Colombian Courts,' *Verfassungsblog.de* (23 February 2023) <https://verfassungsblog.de/colombian-chatgpt/>

36 Brittan Heller and Daniel Castaño, 'Artificial Intelligence, Virtual Courts, and Real Harms,' *Lawfare* (13 March 2023) <https://www.lawfaremedia.org/article/artificial-intelligence-virtual-courts-and-real-harms>.

these guidelines are appropriately followed, there is no reason why generative AI could not be a potentially useful secondary tool.[37] '

SENTENCING AND PROBATION

7.19 In 2001, the UK introduced the Offender Assessment System (OASys) to aid the courts and probation officers in assessing those convicted of crimes[38]. OASys was developed as a 'structured clinical risk assessment tool' for enabling a probation officer or similar suitably qualified individual to better assess:

1 the likelihood of reoffending;

2 whether the convicted person has particular needs directly related to their offence; including personality characteristics or behavioural problems;

3 the risk of serious harm – to the convicted individual, others, etc; and

4 how the risk of such harms can best be managed.[39]

The system is also designed to link assessment of the above to a supervision or sentencing plan, flag the need for further specialist assessment (if applicable), and measure any change in the convicted person's needs during the supervision/sentencing period[40].

7.20 The OASys system provides the courts and probation service with a Offender Group Reconviction Scale (OGRS). This scale uses static factors like age, gender, criminal history etc. to determine a person's likelihood of reoffending within a 12 to 24 months period[41]. The score ranges from 0 to 1 where a lower score correlates with a lower likelihood of reoffending. The system generates a number of other, crime-specific indicators including – but not limited – to: the General reoffending predictor, the Violence Predictor, the Serious Harm assessment, and the Sexual Reoffending Predictor. The General reoffending Predictor (OGP) estimates the likelihood of non-violent reoffending based on static factors (age, criminal record, etc) and dynamic factors (substance abuse, employment, behaviour etc).[42] Non-sexual violent offences are assigned via

37 'Artificial Intelligence (AI) – Judicial Guidance,' *Courts and Tribunals Judiciary* (12 December 2023) <https://www.judiciary.uk/guidance-and-resources/artificial-intelligence-ai-judicial-guidance/>

38 Robin Moore, *A compendium of research and analysis on the Offender Assessment System (OASys): 2009 – 2013,* National Offender Management Service (July 2015) <https://assets.publishing.service.gov.uk/government/uploads/system/uploads/attachment_data/file/449357/research-analysis-offender-assessment-system.pdf>

39 'Incorporate Offender Assessment data to the Justice Data Lab process – Methodology', *Ministry of Justice* (January 2016) <https://assets.publishing.service.gov.uk/government/uploads/system/uploads/attachment_data/file/491688/oasys-methodology.pdf> , p. 4

40 'Incorporate Offender Assessment data to the Justice Data Lab process – Methodology', *Ministry of Justice* (January 2016) <https://assets.publishing.service.gov.uk/government/uploads/system/uploads/attachment_data/file/491688/oasys-methodology.pdf> , p. 4

41 'Incorporate Offender Assessment data to the Justice Data Lab process – Methodology', *Ministry of Justice* (January 2016) <https://assets.publishing.service.gov.uk/government/uploads/system/uploads/attachment_data/file/491688/oasys-methodology.pdf> , p. 4

42 'Offender Management and sentencing planning,' *Prison Reform Trust* (July 2022) <https://prisonreformtrust.org.uk/adviceguide/offender-management-and-sentence-planning/>

the OASys Violence Predictor (OVP); it also uses both dynamic and static factors to assess the likelihood of reoffending[43]. Meanwhile, the Risk of Serious Harm (RoSH) assessment is used to determine if there is risk of serious harm to others, to children, to the individual (suicide or self-harm), or other risks (absconding, control issues etc.)[44]. Unlike the previous two, RoSH categorises offenders into Low, Medium, High, and Very High risk. The OASys Sexual reoffending Predictor (OSP) is used to predict the likelihood that a sexual offender or person convicted of child sexual offences will have a repeat sexual conviction[45].

7.21 Needless to say, the OASys algorithm has significantly impacted how the courts and probation services assess: bail, immigration cases, sentencing, prison security classifications, assignments to rehabilitation programmes, supervision conditions, and early release from custody[46]. For example, whereas a parole officer pre-2001 would have interviewed a defendant in-person to determine whether they were remorseful or potential dangerous, post-2001, much of this casework has been increasingly automated and decisions have been taken purely based on the algorithmic predictions[47].

CONCLUSION: RISKS AND CHALLENGES OF INTEGRATING AI INTO THE UK JUDICIAL SYSTEM

7.22 Despite the considerable benefits the technology offers the profession, the use of AI in UK criminal proceedings presents significant risks that need careful consideration and mitigation. As already intimated throughout this chapter, these risks primarily revolve around fairness, bias, transparency, accuracy, and the fundamental rights of defendants.

1 **Bias and discrimination:**

- **Data bias:** AI algorithms are trained on historical data, which may reflect existing societal biases. If the data used to train a predictive policing algorithm, for example, overrepresents certain ethnic groups in crime statistics, the algorithm might unfairly target those groups, perpetuating discriminatory practices. Similarly, sentencing algorithms trained on biased data could lead to harsher sentences for certain demographics.

43 'Offender Management and sentencing planning,' *Prison Reform Trust* (July 2022) <https://prisonreformtrust.org.uk/adviceguide/offender-management-and-sentence-planning/>

44 'Offender Management and sentencing planning,' *Prison Reform Trust* (July 2022) <https://prisonreformtrust.org.uk/adviceguide/offender-management-and-sentence-planning/>

45 'Offender Management and sentencing planning,' *Prison Reform Trust* (July 2022) <https://prisonreformtrust.org.uk/adviceguide/offender-management-and-sentence-planning/>

46 'Offender Management and sentencing planning,' *Prison Reform Trust* (July 2022) <https://prisonreformtrust.org.uk/adviceguide/offender-management-and-sentence-planning/>

47 Melissa Hamilton and Pamela Ugwudike, 'A 'black box' AI system has been influencing criminal justice decisions for over two decades – it's time to open it up,' *The Conversation* (26 July 2023) <https://theconversation.com/a-black-box-ai-system-has-been-influencing-criminal-justice-decisions-for-over-two-decades-its-time-to-open-it-up-200594>

- **Algorithmic bias:** Even with unbiased data, algorithms themselves can develop biases during the training process. This can result in discriminatory outcomes even when the input data is seemingly neutral.
- **Lack of contextual understanding:** AI lacks the nuanced understanding of human behaviour and social context that a judge or jury possesses. This can lead to misinterpretations of data and potentially unfair judgments.
- **The human-AI fairness gap:** Research shows that public perception sees judgements made by humans as fairer than those made by machines, regardless of the various flaws and biases associated with human decision-making[48].

2 **Transparency and explainability:**

- **'Black box' problem:** Many AI algorithms are opaque in their decision-making processes. This lack of transparency makes it difficult to understand how a particular outcome was reached, raising concerns about due process and the right to a fair trial. It is hard to challenge a decision if you do not understand how it was made.
- **Difficulty in accountability:** If an AI system makes an error or produces a biased outcome, it can be challenging to assign responsibility. Who is liable: the developer of the algorithm, the provider of the data, or the human operator who deployed the system? This lack of clear accountability can erode trust in the justice system.

3 **Privacy and data security:**

- **Sensitive data handling:** Criminal proceedings involve highly sensitive personal data, including criminal records, biometric information, and communications. The use of AI requires robust data security measures to prevent breaches and protect individuals' privacy rights.
- **Data retention and use:** Clear guidelines are needed on how long AI-related data is retained, how it is used, and who has access to it. There is a risk of data being used for purposes beyond its original intent, potentially leading to surveillance and profiling.

4 **Due process and fair trial rights:**

- **Right to a fair hearing:** The use of AI should not infringe upon defendants' right to a fair hearing, including the right to challenge evidence and present a defence. Opaque AI systems can make it difficult to exercise these rights effectively.
- **Presumption of innocence:** The use of predictive policing or risk assessment tools should not undermine the presumption of innocence. Individuals should not be treated as guilty based solely on algorithmic predictions.

48 John Roberts, *Year-End Report on the Federal Judiciary* (2023) US Supreme Court.gov <https://www.supremecourt.gov/publicinfo/year-end/2023year-endreport.pdf> , pp. 6

5 **Access to justice and equality:**

- **Cost and availability:** Sophisticated AI tools can be expensive, potentially creating an uneven playing field between well-resourced prosecution teams and defendants with limited means. This could exacerbate existing inequalities in access to justice.
- **Digital literacy:** Understanding and interacting with AI-driven systems requires a certain level of digital literacy. Individuals lacking these skills may be disadvantaged in navigating the legal process.

Conclusion

Chapter 8

The future of AI in criminal proceedings

8.01 On 1 May 2024, *The Times* reported that 'the legal industry is likely to be the second most impacted by AI, with 46 percent of tasks able to be automated by this technology[1].' Meanwhile, a recent survey conducted by LexisNexis (in 2024), revealed that 82% of legal practitioners in the UK – one-in-four – already use or plan to use GenAI in their practice[2]. Large legal firms have largely paved the way with 78% having implemented GenAI; in-house legal counsel have also been early adopters with 74% integrating AI into their workstreams[3]. Meanwhile, at the Bar of England and Wales the number of practitioners using GenAI in their practice has jumped from 8% to 32% in 2024[4].

8.02 Given these startling figures, it seemed appropriate to ask Vertex AI (by Google) how AI will impact UK criminal lawyers in the next 5–10 years. We have amended and amplified the output to make it more helpful for readers, which emphasises how AI output must be used at the moment given the current state of the technology[5]:

> *AI's impact on UK criminal lawyers in the next 5-10 years will be transformative, presenting both opportunities and significant challenges.*
>
> *Opportunities for Criminal Lawyers:*
>
> - ***Enhanced Investigative Capabilities[6]:*** *AI's ability to analyse crime data and identify patterns could influence policing strategies and resource allocation. AI-powered systems can analyse vast amounts of data (eg, CCTV footage, social media posts, police reports) to identify patterns, locate witnesses, and uncover hidden connections much faster than human investigators. While not directly impacting lawyers' daily work, this could affect the*

1 'Why it's time for law firms to start investing in generative AI,' (1 May 2024) *The Times UK* <https://www.thetimes.com/static/law-firms-tech-generative-ai-risks-research/>

2 Dylan Brown, 'AI Adoption soars across UK legal sector,' (25 September 2024) *LexisNexis* <https://www.lexisnexis.co.uk/blog/future-of-law/ai-adoption-soars-across-uk-legal-sector>

3 Dylan Brown, 'AI Adoption soars across UK legal sector,' (25 September 2024) *LexisNexis* <https://www.lexisnexis.co.uk/blog/future-of-law/ai-adoption-soars-across-uk-legal-sector>

4 Dylan Brown, 'AI Adoption soars across UK legal sector,' (25 September 2024) *LexisNexis* <https://www.lexisnexis.co.uk/blog/future-of-law/ai-adoption-soars-across-uk-legal-sector>

5 Manish Garg, 'All you need to know about AI adoption in Criminal Justice,' (25 June 2024) *TechUK.org* < *https://www.techuk.org/resource/all-you-need-to-know-about-ai-adoption-in-criminal-justice.html*>

6 Manish Garg, 'All you need to know about AI adoption in Criminal Justice,' (25 June 2024) TechUK.org < https://www.techuk.org/resource/all-you-need-to-know-about-ai-adoption-in-criminal-justice.html>

types of cases they handle. This being said, the technology could lead to more efficient and thorough investigations, potentially resulting in a higher rate of successful prosecutions.

- ***Improved Case Preparation[7]:*** *AI can automate tasks like legal research, document review, and the identification of relevant precedents, significantly reducing the time and effort required for case preparation. This allows lawyers to focus on developing stronger legal strategies and client interaction. Moreover, tools that analyse large volumes of legal documents and evidence will become increasingly sophisticated.*
- ***Data-Driven Insights & Decision Support:*** *AI-powered predictive analytics can help lawyers assess the strengths and weaknesses of a case, predict the likelihood of success, and optimise legal strategies. This can assist lawyers in making more informed decisions about case strategy, plea bargaining, and sentencing. However, this necessitates a critical understanding of the limitations and potential biases in AI predictions.*
- ***Improved Client Communication[8]:*** *AI chatbots could offer 24/7 client support, providing basic legal information and addressing routine queries, freeing up lawyers' time for more complex issues.*
- ***Virtual Courtrooms and Proceedings[9]:*** *AI could facilitate the development of virtual courtrooms, streamlining administrative tasks and potentially reducing the need for physical appearances in court. This would have implications for how lawyers prepare and present their cases.*
- **New Jobs Centred Around Effective GenAI Use[10]:** it is likely new careers will emerge in legal engineering – people tasked with managing AI systems for legal practices, with generating AI systems specifically trained on jurisdiction-specific legal data, for example. There will likely also be in-house roles for legal engineers; they will be responsible for prompt engineering to ensure that prompts used by legal practitioners and staff are as effective and accurate as possible.

Challenges for Criminal Lawyers:

- ***Algorithmic Bias and Fairness:*** *AI systems are only as good as the data they are trained on. If the data reflects existing societal biases (eg, racial or socioeconomic biases), the AI system will perpetuate and potentially amplify these biases, leading to unfair outcomes. This raises serious ethical concerns, particularly in criminal justice, where decisions can have life-altering consequences. Criminal lawyers will need to challenge the use of biased algorithms and ensure fair application of AI technology. Questions about data privacy, algorithmic bias, and the potential for misinterpretation of AI-generated information will be central to this discussion.*

7 Stu White, 'How AI is reshaping the future of legal practice,' (20 November 2024) *The Law Society* <https://www.lawsociety.org.uk/topics/ai-and-lawtech/partner-content/how-ai-is-reshaping-the-future-of-legal-practice>

8 Lena Haffner, 'The power of legal AI chatbots,' (26 March 2024) *Norton Rose Fulbright* <https://connections.nortonrosefulbright.com/post/102j3q3/the-power-of-legal-ai-chatbots>

9 Exploring the Impact of Virtual and Augmented REality in Courts,' (21 July 2023) *UNESCO.org* <https://www.unesco.org/en/articles/exploring-impact-virtual-and-augmented-reality-courts>

10 Source: Sterling Miller, 'The future of artificial intelligence: Robots are coming – or are they?' (2024) *Thomson Reuters Legal* <https://legal.thomsonreuters.com/en/insights/articles/future-of-artificial-intelligence-robot-lawyer-army-or-not>

- ***Risk Assessment Tools and Due Process:*** *The use of AI-driven risk assessment tools in determining bail, sentencing, or parole decisions raises concerns about due process and fairness . These tools often lack transparency and may not adequately account for individual circumstances, potentially leading to wrongful detention or harsher sentences.*
- ***Transparency and Explainability:*** *Many AI systems, particularly deep learning models, are 'black boxes,' making it difficult to understand how they arrive at their decisions. This lack of transparency poses significant challenges for legal defence, as lawyers may struggle to understand and challenge the AI's reasoning.*
- ***Job Displacement Concerns:*** *Automation of routine tasks could lead to job displacement for some paralegals and junior lawyers.*

We are already witnessing the rise of robo-lawyers, AI chatbots capable of representing clients in simple proceedings such as overturning parking fines[11].

- ***Need for New Skills[12]:*** *Lawyers will need to adapt and develop new skills to effectively utilise AI tools in their practice. This may involve learning how to use specific software, understanding the limitations of AI, and interpreting AI-generated insights.*
- ***Digital Divide:*** *Unequal access to AI tools between the prosecution and the defence, or between well-funded and less-funded agencies, could create an imbalance in the justice system. This could disadvantage defendants represented by less well-resourced lawyers.*
- ***Changing Roles[13]:*** *The role of criminal lawyers may evolve, with less emphasis on routine tasks and more focus on strategic thinking, creative problem-solving, and client counselling.*

OTHER PROCEDURAL AND SUBSTANTIVE ISSUES THAT MAY ARISE FROM USING AI

8.03 The growing use of LLMs is already changing the way in which discovery is being conducted during proceedings. As GenAI becomes increasingly embedded in legal procedures, LLMs are likely to challenge existing evidentiary and procedural rules; courts will be faced with decisions such as whether to admit evidence that is wholly or partially generated by an AI system and new procedures may have to be developed to regulate this type of evidence, particularly given the sophistication of deepfakes[14]. It is likely that heavily regulated industries – eg banking and finance – will prohibit or severely restrict the use of AI-generated documents and other evidence.

11 This chatbot is called 'DoNotPay' and, while it has had some success in litigation of this sort, it has also been hit with a range of lawsuits – including, practising without a licence. See: Sara Merken, 'Lawsuit pits class action firm against 'robot lawyer' DoNotPay (9 March 2023) *Reuters.com* <https://www.reuters.com/legal/lawsuit-pits-class-action-firm-against-robot-lawyer-donotpay-2023-03-09/>

12 Jane Wang and Sharyn Ch'ang, 'Are you using AI yet? How lawyers can use it to their advantage,' (September 2023) *Pwc.com* <https://www.pwc.com/gx/en/about/pwc-asia-pacific/are-you-using-ai-yet-how-lawyers-can-use-it-to-their-advantage.html>

13 Bernard Marr, 'How Generative AI Will Change the Jobs of Lawyers,' (14 March 2024) *Forbes.com* <https://www.forbes.com/sites/bernardmarr/2024/03/14/how-generative-ai-will-change-the-jobs-of-lawyers/>

14 'The key legal issues relating to the use, acquisition, and development of AI,' (1 March 2024) *Thomson Reuters Legal* <https://legal.thomsonreuters.com/blog/the-key-legal-issues-with-gen-ai/#procedural-and-substantive-issues>

8.04 In the near future, GenAI is likely to instigate a wave of substantive issues in litigation proceedings in a variety of fields of legal practice, including: data privacy claims, theft/fraud, and defamation[15]. It is also likely that professional negligence claims, disciplinary proceedings and/or appeals will arise from individuals claiming their solicitor/barrister/ legal advisor/ employers etc misused or inadequately used GenAI. Indeed, before AI-in-law was even a trend, the Post Office Horizon scandal has demonstrated the dangers and legal consequences of undisclosed bugs in automated systems[16]. In terms of professional negligence claims specifically, these might arise from any of the following (this is a non-exhaustive list): the legal representative's failure to adequately audit the GenAI's output; a failure to use sufficiently comprehensive prompts; a failure to ensure the LLM used was the best suited for the legal representative's/client's purpose; and a failure to disclose to the client that a GenAI was used in the researching and/or drafting of their legal advice.

LITIGANTS IN PERSON AND ACCESS TO JUSTICE

8.05 Many experts believe AI can improve access to justice, particularly in its ability to simplify legal procedures and paperwork – not to mention jargon and expenses – for litigants in person. However, the technology is currently too nascent for *carte-blanche* real-world deployment. For example, in December 2023, a litigant in person (LIP) sought to rely on nine authorities in her appeal against HMRC; all nine were found to be fictitious 'hallucinations'[17].

8.06 However, online legal databases are integrating natural language processing (NLP) into their architectures meaning integration of GenAI is not far off. As shown in Chapter 6, the likes of Westlaw and LexisNexis already use LLMs to answer basic legal questions and NLPs to match a user's search to relevant words and phrases in documents to provide the most relevant results[18].

AI IN/AS A COURT

8.07 This brings us to our next point: AI will eventually reach sufficient levels of sophistication that it will be capable of acting autonomously on behalf of a client, in court or in providing legal advice on the papers. After all, Chat-GPT already has voice functionality; once the technology becomes more reliable and privacy-orientated, there will be no real technological barriers to an LIP asking it to provide submissions in court on their behalf. This reality is not as far off as you may first imagine: Chat-GPT 4 passed the US Bar Exam in 2023, scoring in the 90th

15 'The key legal issues relating to the use, acquisition, and development of AI,' (1 March 2024) *Thomson Reuters Legal* <https://legal.thomsonreuters.com/blog/the-key-legal-issues-with-gen-ai/#procedural-and-substantive-issues>
16 'Post Office Horizon scandal: Why hundreds were wrongly prosecuted,' (30 July 2024) *BBC News* <https://www.bbc.co.uk/news/business-56718036>
17 Felicity Harber v The Commissioners for HMRC [2023] UKFTT 1007 (TC)
18 Andrew Judkins, 'Use of AI in litigation: A quick look at today and the future,' *Norton Rose Fulbright* (5 October 2023) <https://www.nortonrosefulbright.com/en/inside-disputes/blog/use-of-ai-in-litigation-a-quick-look-at-today-and-the-future>

percentile with a 75% accuracy rate, higher than the 68% human average[19]. The experiment, run by researchers at the Illinois Institute of Technology, demonstrates that ML and GenAI can already perform complex legal tasks and provide legal answers that are 'representative good answers' to many state bar exams in the US.[20]

8.08 This raises the pressing question of liability, a question that has long plagued other industries such as the automotive industry (self-driving cars) and bioengineering (AI powered surgical equipment). Who is responsible when an AI system gives disastrous legal advice? The legal practitioner deploying the AI? The purchaser of the AI system (if different from the deployer)? The developer? The individual engineer who worked on the model itself? The training data provider (if different from the AI system developer)? Will legal practices be required to buy insurance when they purchase a legal AI model? Should they?

8.09 Even if this scenario does not materialise and the adoption of AI is less universal, the legal process in England and Wales will undoubtedly be required to incorporate expertise regarding whether or not an AI has functioned adequately or not[21]. This component of the procedural framework will be intrinsic to complex AI-related cases and/or cases in which AI was used to partly or wholly generate evidentiary materials.

8.10 For the judges' part, Master of the Rolls, Sir Geoffrey Vos, recently stated that machines (namely, AI) will eventually be used to make decisions in 'less intensely personal disputes' in the UK[22]. His prediction is supported by the fact that globally, judiciaries are relying on AI to adjudicate matters, particularly in civil courts (see Chapter 7). Admittedly, however, he does not believe they will be trusted by the public to deal with more complex or emotionally charged matters such as disputes involving children or murder trials.

CONCLUSION

8.11 Broadly speaking, AI has the potential to alter the practice of criminal law in the UK. Criminal lawyers must proactively engage with these technologies to understand both their potential benefits and inherent risks. Developing expertise in AI ethics, data analysis, and algorithmic accountability will be essential for ensuring fair outcomes in the criminal justice system. Advocacy for transparent and unbiased AI systems will also be vital for maintaining the integrity of the legal process and preventing the perpetuation of existing inequalities.

19 Katz, Daniel Martin and Bommarito, Michael James and Gao, Shang and Arredondo, Pablo, GPT-4 Passes the Bar Exam (March 15, 2023). 382 Philosophical Transactions of the Royal Society A (2024), http://dx.doi.org/10.2139/ssrn.4389233

20 'GPT-4 Passes the Bar Exam', *Illinois Tech.edu* (15 March 2023) <https://www.iit.edu/news/gpt-4-passes-bar-exam>

21 Keri Grieman, 'Judge Dread: AI and Judicial Integrity,' (2021) *United Nations Office on Drugs and Crime* <https://www.unodc.org/dohadeclaration/en/news/2021/30/judge-dread_ai-and-judicial-integrity.html>

22 Sir Geoffrey Vos, 'Speech by the Master of the Rolls to the Law Society of Scotland,' (14 June 2023) *Courts and Tribunals Judiciary* <https://www.judiciary.uk/speech-by-the-master-of-the-rolls-to-the-law-society-of-scotland/> at [22]

8.12 However, it is important to note that the adoption and impact of AI in the UK criminal justice system will be influenced by factors such as regulation, funding, and public acceptance. As of February 2025, these factors are still evolving, and the predictions presented here are subject to change.

Index

References are to paragraph number.

Bloomsbury Professional Law Insight

AI in Criminal Law